Fancy Tea: A Guide to Non-Alcoholic Tea Cocktails

Enjoy your loose leaf tea like you never did before

Tanja Boldt

Copyright © 2023 by Tanja Boldt
All rights reserved.
ISBN: 978-0-6459486-1-5 (Paperback)
978-0-6459486-2-2 (Hardcover)

Table Of Contents

Chapter 1 Welcome to the World of Non-Alcoholic Tea Cocktails   1

    How to Use this Guide   5

Chapter 2 Tea Basics   9

    Understanding Tea Varieties   10

    Black Tea   11

    Green Tea   13

    White Tea   14

    Herbal Tea   16

    Brewing the Perfect Cup of Tea   19

    Water Temperature and Steeping Times   20

    Tea Brewing Tools and Techniques   22

Chapter 3 Tea Cocktails   25

    The Art of Mixology   26

    Essential Ingredients for Tea Cocktails   27

    Tools for Tea Cocktail Making   29

    Proper Glassware for Serving   31

Chapter 4 Classic Non-Alcoholic Tea Cocktails   35

    Earl Grey Sunrise recipe   36

    Matcha Mojito   37

Hibiscus Margarita	39
Purple Island (with blue pea butterfly and lemon)	41
Jasmine Lemonade	43
Goddess Spritzer-Herbal Heaven	45
Chapter 5 Tea Mocktails for Tealovers	**49**
Minty Iced Tea Punch	50
Lemongrass and Ginger Refresher	52
Tropical Tea Cooler	54
Spiced Apple Chai Mocktail	55
Lavender Lemon Fizz	57
Cherry Berry Iced Tea	60
Chapter 6 Tea Cocktails for Parents and Kids	**63**
Fruity Tea Popsicles	64
Blue Magic Iced Tea (Blue Pea Butterfly Flower)	65
Tea-infused Smoothies	67
Sparkling Tea Floats	69
Tea-based Slushies	71
Tea Milkshakes	72
Chapter 7 Exploring Unique Tea Flavours	**75**
Rose-infused Tea Cocktails	76
Ginger and Turmeric Tea Blends	78
Exotic Fruit Tea Cocktails	79
Herbal Infusions for Mocktails	81
Floral Tea Elixirs	83

Chapter 8 Health Benefits of Non-Alcoholic Tea Cocktails	87
Antioxidant-rich Tea Varieties	88
Digestive and Calming Properties	90
Boosting Energy and Immunity	91
Promoting Mental Well-being	93
Supporting Weight Management	95
Chapter 9 Hosting Tea Cocktail Parties	99
Setting the Ambience	100
Tea Cocktail Pairings with Food	101
Mocktail Stations and Bar Setups	103
Tea Cocktails Party Themes	105
Tips for a Successful Tea Cocktail Party	107
Chapter 10 Conclusion and Final Thoughts	109
Embracing the World of Non-Alcoholic Tea Cocktails	110
Experimenting with Your Own Creations	112
Savoring the Joy of Sipping Tea Cocktails	114
Appendix:	117
Glossary of Tea Terms	118
Resources for Tea Ingredients and Accessories	119
Tea Cocktail Recipes Index	122

01

Chapter 1: Welcome to the World of Non-Alcoholic Tea Cocktails

Fancy Tea: A Guide to Non-Alcoholic Tea Cocktails

In recent years, we've witnessed an incredible transformation in the world of mixology. Cocktails, traditionally associated with alcoholic beverages, have given rise to a captivating new trend that is captivating the beverage industry - the glorious world of non-alcoholic mixology. This section is all about delving into this exciting phenomenon and its impact on tea enthusiasts, parents, kids, teetotalers and those seeking healthier drink options. Let's embark on this delightful journey together! Non-alcoholic mixology is the art of crafting exquisite and sophisticated cocktails without the use of alcohol. Instead, these beverages are created using a variety of ingredients, with tea taking centre stage as a versatile and flavourful base. The popularity of non-alcoholic mixology can be attributed to a multitude of factors, including the growing interest in health-conscious choices, the desire for unique and creative drink options and the need for inclusive social gatherings. Tea lovers, rejoice! Loose-leaf tea has found a new purpose in the world of non-alcoholic mixology. With its diverse range of flavours, aromas and health benefits, tea provides an excellent foundation for crafting tantalizing mocktails. From floral and fruity infusions to robust and earthy brews, there is a tea for every taste preference. Imagine sipping on a Lavender Lemonade Spritzer or a Hibiscus Mojito, both infused with the goodness of tea. The possibilities are endless. Parents and kids can also revel in the non-alcoholic mixology trend. Gone are the days when children were limited to sugary sodas and artificially flavoured drinks. Now, parents can introduce their little ones to a world of sophisticated, non-alcoholic beverages that stimulate their taste buds and nourish their bodies. Tea mocktails offer a healthier alternative to traditional soft drinks, providing hydration, antioxidants and a burst of flavour in every sip. For those who choose not to consume alcohol, non-alcoholic mixology offers a refreshing and inclusive alternative. Whether it's due to personal preference, health reasons or cultural beliefs, everyone deserves the opportunity to enjoy a well-crafted beverage.

Non-alcoholic cocktails, with their intricate flavour profiles and beautiful presentation, allow individuals to partake in social gatherings without feeling left out or compromising their choices.

Moreover, non-alcoholic mixology aligns perfectly with the growing demand for healthier drink choices. As people become more conscious of their overall well-being, they seek alternatives that nourish their bodies, without sacrificing taste. Tea-based mocktails are an ideal solution, offering a myriad of health benefits while still providing a delightful drinking experience.

The rise of non-alcoholic mixology has revolutionized the way we approach beverages. Through the use of loose- leaf tea as a base, this trend has opened up a world of possibilities for tea lovers, parents, kids, individuals abstaining from alcohol and those seeking healthier drink choices. So, raise your glass and embrace the art of non-alcoholic mixology – a delightful journey that tantalizes the taste buds, nourishes the body and fosters inclusivity.

1. Tea cocktails provide a healthier alternative to alcoholic beverages, without compromising on taste. They are packed with antioxidants, vitamins and minerals that promote overall well- being. For example, green tea cocktails help boost metabolism, black tea cocktails aid digestion and herbal tea cocktails soothe the senses and promote relaxation.

2. Versatility and Flavour: Non-alcoholic tea cocktails offer an endless array of flavours and combinations. From fruity infusions to exotic blends, these teas can be mixed with various ingredients like fresh fruits, herbs and spices. The result is a tantalizing burst of flavours that cater to different palates. Whether you prefer a zesty citrus blend or a calming lavender infusion, there is a non- alcoholic tea cocktail to suit every taste.

Fancy Tea: A Guide to Non-Alcoholic Tea Cocktails

3. All-Age Appeal: One of the most significant advantages of non-alcoholic tea cocktails is their inclusivity. These beverages can be enjoyed by people of all ages, making them perfect for family gatherings, parties or when hosting friends. Parents can share the joy of sipping a delicious tea cocktail with their children, fostering a sense of togetherness and creating lasting memories.

4. Social Elegance: Fancy tea cocktails elevate any occasion with their elegance and sophistication. Their vibrant colours, beautiful garnishes and enticing aromas make them a visual delight. Whether you are hosting a high tea party or enjoying a quiet evening at home, non-alcoholic tea cocktails add a touch of refinement and make any gathering more memorable.

5. Responsible Choice: For those who choose not to consume alcohol, non- alcoholic tea cocktails offer a responsible and enjoyable alternative. They provide a refreshing beverage option that allows individuals to participate in social gatherings without compromising their personal choices or values.

In conclusion, non-alcoholic tea cocktails offer a plethora of benefits for tea lovers, parents, kids and those seeking healthier drink choices. With their health benefits, versatility, all-age appeal, social elegance and responsible nature, these fancy tea concoctions are a delightful addition to any beverage repertoire. So, sip, savour and indulge in the world of non-alcoholic tea cocktails, and discover a new realm of flavours, aromas and well-being.

How to Use this Guide

Welcome to 'Fancy Tea: A Guide to Non-Alcoholic Tea Cocktails'! This subchapter is designed to help you navigate through this book and make the most out of your tea cocktail experience. Whether you are a tea lover, a parent, someone who doesn't drink alcohol or simply searching for healthier drink choices, this guide is tailored to meet your needs.

1. Understanding the Basics: Before diving into the world of non-alcoholic tea cocktails, it's essential to grasp the basics of tea brewing, ingredients and flavour profiles. This section will provide you with a solid foundation to build upon.

2. Exploring Different Tea Varieties: In this chapter, we'll delve into the diverse world of tea. From black and green teas to herbal and fruit infusions, you'll discover the unique characteristics and flavour profiles of each variety. This knowledge will help you choose the perfect teas for your cocktails.

3. The Art of Tea Mixing: Mixing tea with other ingredients is an art form that requires creativity and experimentation. We'll guide you through the process of creating balanced and flavourful tea cocktails, ensuring that each sip is a delight to the senses.

4. Health Benefits of Tea: Tea is not only a delicious beverage but also offers numerous health benefits. From boosting immunity to improving digestion, we'll explore the positive impacts of tea on your overall well-being. This section is particularly useful for health-conscious individuals.

5. Tea Mocktail Recipes: Get ready to embark on a journey filled with tantalizing tea mocktail recipes. From classic favourites with a twist to innovative creations, we've curated a collection of beverages that will satisfy even the most discerning palate. Each recipe includes detailed instructions and ingredient variations to suit your preferences.

6. Tea Pairing Suggestions: Pairing tea cocktails with food can elevate your sensory experience. In this section, we'll provide recommendations and tips for pairing your tea mocktails with different cuisines and occasions. From afternoon tea parties to family gatherings, we've got you covered.

7. Tips for Hosting Tea Cocktail Parties: If you're looking to impress your guests with a fancy tea cocktail soirée, this chapter will guide you through hosting a memorable event. From setting the ambience to

crafting a stunning beverage menu, these tips and tricks will ensure your party is a resounding success.

So, grab your teacup, sharpen your mixology skills and join us on this flavourful journey. 'Fancy Tea' is your ultimate companion for discovering the world of non-alcoholic tea cocktails, making healthier drink choices and indulging in the art of tea. Let's raise a teacup and toast to a delightful experience!

02

Chapter 2: Tea Basics

Understanding Tea Varieties

Tea has been enjoyed for centuries around the world and its popularity continues to grow, especially among tea lovers, parents, kids, people who don't drink alcohol and those looking for healthier drink choices. In the realm of fancy tea, a wide variety of options await those who seek a refined and pleasurable tea-drinking experience. This subchapter aims to provide a comprehensive understanding of the different tea varieties available, allowing you to explore the world of fancy tea and select the perfect cup for any occasion.

Green Tea: Renowned for its delicate flavour and health benefits, green tea is unoxidized and offers a fresh, grassy taste. Rich in antioxidants, it is believed to aid in weight loss, improve brain function and reduce the risk of heart disease. Its vibrant green colour and mild flavour make it an excellent choice for tea enthusiasts of all ages.

Black Tea: The most robust and fully oxidized tea variety, black tea boasts a strong flavour profile with hints of malt and earthiness. Often enjoyed with milk or sugar, it provides a stimulating caffeine boost. Black tea is perfect for a morning pick-me-up or a relaxing afternoon tea break.

White Tea: Known for its delicate and subtle taste, white tea is minimally processed and contains the least amount of caffeine among all tea types. It offers a light and refreshing experience, with floral and fruity notes. White tea is a great choice for those who prefer a milder taste and are looking for a caffeine-light option.

Herbal Tea: While not technically tea, herbal infusions are popular among those seeking caffeine-free alternatives. With a wide range of flavours and health benefits, herbal teas include chamomile, peppermint, hibiscus and many more. They are often enjoyed for their calming effects, digestive properties or simply as an enjoyable and soothing beverage.

Oolong Tea: Falling between green and black tea in terms of oxidation, oolong tea offers a unique balance of flavours. With a range from light and floral to rich and toasty, oolong tea provides a diverse taste experience. Its caffeine content varies depending on the specific variety, making it suitable for both daytime and evening sipping.

By understanding the different tea varieties available, you can elevate your tea- drinking experience and explore the world of fancy tea. Whether you're a tea lover, a parent looking for healthier drink choices for your kids or someone who prefers non-alcoholic options, there's a tea variety out there to suit your taste and preferences. So, sit back, sip and savour the delightful world of tea. Cheers to a healthier and more enjoyable tea experience!

Black Tea

Black tea, the most popular type of tea in the world, is known for its robust flavour and rich aroma. It is a favourite among tea lovers due to its versatility and numerous health benefits. In this subchapter, we will explore the wonders of black tea and how it can be incorporated into non-alcoholic tea cocktails for a delightful and healthier drinking experience.

Black tea is derived from the leaves of the Camellia sinensis plant and undergoes a process of withering, rolling, oxidation and drying. This oxidation process gives black tea its distinct flavour and colour. The resulting brew is a dark amber hue with a bold and full-bodied taste that is both refreshing and invigorating.

For tea lovers, black tea offers a wide range of options to suit individual preferences. From classic blends, like English Breakfast and Earl Grey, to specialty teas, like Darjeeling and Assam, there is a black tea for every palate. Its versatility also extends to its ability to be infused with various flavours such as fruits, spices and flowers, making it a perfect base for non-alcoholic tea cocktails.

Parents and kids can enjoy the goodness of black tea without worrying about the negative effects of alcohol. These tea cocktails can be a great alternative to sugary sodas and artificial beverages, providing a healthier option for the whole family. By incorporating fresh fruits, herbs and natural sweeteners, these tea cocktails become not only delicious but also packed with vitamins and antioxidants.

For those seeking a fancy tea experience, black tea can elevate your tea cocktail game to new heights. The bold flavour of black tea pairs well with a variety of ingredients such as citrus fruits, ginger, mint and even exotic floral notes. From a zesty Lemon Ginger Fizz to a fragrant Lavender Earl Grey Spritzer, the possibilities are endless when it comes to creating fancy and sophisticated non-alcoholic tea cocktails with black tea.

Whether you are a tea enthusiast, a health-conscious individual or someone looking for a non-alcoholic beverage option, black tea is a delightful choice. Its robust flavour, versatility and numerous health benefits make it an excellent base for non-alcoholic tea cocktails. So, grab your teapot, steep a cup of black tea and embark on a journey of sipping and savouring the wonders of this beloved tea variety.

Green Tea

Green Tea: A Healthful and Refreshing Choice for Tea Lovers.

For centuries, green tea has been celebrated for its numerous health benefits and unique flavours. In this subchapter, we will explore the wonders of green tea, its origins and how to incorporate it into delicious non-alcoholic tea cocktails. Whether you are a tea lover, a parent searching for healthier drink choices for your kids or someone who prefers alcohol-free options, green tea is a fantastic choice that will satisfy your taste buds.

Originating in China, green tea is made from the leaves of the Camellia sinensis plant. It undergoes minimal oxidation during processing, which helps retain its natural antioxidants and vibrant green colour. Packed with polyphenols, vitamins and minerals, green tea is known for its potential health benefits, such as boosting metabolism, improving brain function and reducing the risk of heart disease.

Incorporating green tea into non-alcoholic tea cocktails is a wonderful way to enjoy its flavours and reap its healthful qualities. Whether you prefer a classic green tea infusion or a more elaborate blend, the possibilities are endless. Try combining green tea with fresh fruits like strawberries or peaches for a refreshing and fruity twist. For a floral touch, infuse green tea with lavender or rose petals. You can also experiment with adding herbs like mint or basil to enhance the flavour profile.

For parents seeking healthier drink choices for their children, green tea can be a great alternative to sugary beverages. It provides a natural and delicious option that kids will enjoy, while also introducing them to the world of tea. Serve green tea over ice with a squeeze of lemon or a splash of apple juice for a tasty and nutritious treat.

As part of the Fancy Tea niche, green tea is a staple in elegant tea parties and sophisticated gatherings. Its delicate flavours and vibrant colour make it a perfect base for creating intricate tea cocktails. From a Matcha Mojito to a Green Tea Martini, the possibilities for indulging in fancy tea creations are endless.

In conclusion, green tea is a versatile and healthful choice for tea lovers, parents and those seeking alcohol-free options. Its rich history, potential health benefits and endless flavour combinations make it an excellent addition to any non-alcoholic tea cocktail repertoire. So, go ahead, sip and savour the wonders of green tea in all its glory.

White Tea

White tea is a delicate and elegant beverage that has been enjoyed for centuries. Known for its light and subtle flavour, it is often referred to as the 'Champagne of teas'. In this subchapter, we will explore the origins, health benefits and various ways to enjoy this exquisite tea.

Originating from the Fujian province in China, white tea is made from the youngest leaves and buds of the Camellia sinensis plant. These leaves are carefully handpicked and gently dried, preserving their natural flavour and nutrients. The minimal processing involved in producing white tea results in a pale golden liquor with a delicate aroma.

One of the most appealing aspects of white tea is its numerous health benefits. Rich in antioxidants, it helps combat free radicals in the body, reducing the risk of chronic diseases. The high levels of catechins found in white tea also boost the immune system and promote cardiovascular health. Additionally, studies have shown that white tea may aid in weight management and improve skin health.

For tea lovers seeking a non-alcoholic alternative, white tea is an excellent choice. Its low caffeine content makes it a suitable beverage for individuals looking to limit their caffeine intake. White tea can be enjoyed hot or cold, making it a versatile option for any occasion.

Parents interested in introducing healthier drink choices to their children will find white tea to be an ideal option. With its naturally sweet and mild taste, it is a refreshing alternative to sugary sodas and juices. White tea can be infused with fruits or herbs to create enticing mocktails that kids will love.

White tea is also a favourite among those who appreciate fancy tea. Its subtle flavour and delicate appearance make it a perfect choice for afternoon tea parties or elegant gatherings. Pair it with scones, pastries or light sandwiches for a truly sophisticated experience.

In conclusion, white tea is a sophisticated, healthy and versatile beverage that caters to a wide range of individuals. Whether you are a tea lover, a parent seeking healthier options for your children or someone looking for fancy tea choices, white tea is sure to delight your palate and provide a refreshing alternative to alcoholic cocktails. So, sip and savour the beauty of white tea, and let its subtle flavours transport you to a world of elegance and tranquillity.

Herbal Tea

Herbal Tea: Discover the Delights of Nature's Brews

Welcome to the world of herbal tea, where nature's bounty infuses your cup with delightful flavours and soothing aromas. In this subchapter, we delve into the realm of herbal teas, exploring their unique characteristics, health benefits and the wide array of options available to tea lovers, parents, kids and anyone seeking healthier drink choices. Whether you're a seasoned tea connoisseur or a curious beginner, prepare to be captivated by the wonders of herbal infusions.

Herbal tea, also known as tisane, is a beverage made from the infusion or decoction of herbs, flowers, fruits or other plant materials that do not contain the Camellia sinensis plant. This means that herbal teas are naturally caffeine-free, making them a perfect choice for those who prefer to avoid or limit their intake of this stimulant. With an endless variety of flavours and medicinal properties, herbal teas offer a world of possibilities for those seeking a healthier alternative to traditional tea or alcohol-based drinks.

For the loose-leaf tea enthusiasts, herbal blends can be transformed into exquisite non-alcoholic tea cocktails, offering a sophisticated and refreshing twist to your beverage repertoire. Imagine sipping on a lavender-infused mocktail or a zesty hibiscus and citrus cooler – herbal teas provide endless opportunities for creative mixology, allowing you to impress guests or simply indulge in a moment of luxury for yourself.

Parents and kids alike can benefit from the gentle and natural goodness of herbal teas. From soothing chamomile to calming lavender, these caffeine-free drinks can help promote relaxation and sleep, making them a wonderful addition to bedtime routines. Additionally, herbal teas can be a flavourful and hydrating alternative to sugary sodas or juices, encouraging healthier choices for the whole family.

For those looking to embrace a healthier lifestyle, herbal teas offer a myriad of health benefits. Each herbal infusion boasts its own unique properties, ranging from boosting the immune system to aiding digestion, reducing inflammation or providing antioxidant support. From classic blends like peppermint and ginger to lesser-known treasures like nettle or rooibos, there is a herbal tea to suit every taste and wellness goal.

So, embark on a journey of discovery and let herbal tea enchant your senses. Explore the world of flavours, aromas and health benefits that await you in every cup. Whether you're seeking a soothing bedtime ritual, a fancy mocktail for a special occasion or a healthier alternative to alcohol, herbal tea has something to offer everyone. Sip, savour and enjoy the wonders of nature's brews.

Brewing the Perfect Cup of Tea

Tea is not just a beverage, it's a ritual, a moment of calm in our busy lives. For tea lovers, brewing the perfect cup is an art form, a way to savour the exquisite flavours and fragrances that tea has to offer. In this subchapter, we will dive into the secrets of brewing the perfect cup of tea, ensuring that every sip is a delightful experience.

1. Choosing the Right Tea: Loose-leaf tea lovers know that the quality of the tea leaves is paramount. Opt for loose-leaf tea instead of tea bags, as it allows the leaves to unfurl and release their flavours fully. Explore different varieties such as black, green, white, oolong and herbal teas to find your preference. Each type has its unique characteristics that cater to different taste buds.

Water Temperature and Steeping Time: Achieving the ideal water temperature is crucial for extracting the best flavours from the tea leaves. Different types of tea require different temperatures. For delicate white and green teas, use water that is around 160 to 175°F or 70 to 80°C. Black and herbal teas, on the other hand, fare better with boiling water at around 212°F or 100°C. Steeping times can vary too, typically ranging from 1 to 5 minutes. Experiment with different steeping times to find your desired strength.

2. Tea Accessories: To enhance your tea experience, invest in some fancy tea accessories. A good-quality teapot with a built-in infuser allows the leaves to unfurl and infuse properly. Teacups and saucers add an elegant touch to your tea-drinking ritual. Additionally, a tea timer can help ensure you steep your tea for just the right amount of time.

3. Tea Pairings: Tea can be so much more than just a stand-alone beverage. Consider pairing your tea with complementary flavours. For example, a light and floral green tea pairs wonderfully with citrusy flavours, while a robust black tea can be enjoyed with a slice of chocolate cake. Experiment with different combinations to discover your own unique tea pairings.

4. Health Benefits: Tea is not only a delicious drink but also a healthy choice. It is packed with antioxidants and can help boost immunity, aid digestion, reduce stress and promote relaxation. By opting for tea over alcohol or sugary drinks, you can enjoy a beverage that is not only tasty but also nourishing for your body.

Whether you are a tea enthusiast, a parent looking for healthier drink choices for your family or someone who doesn't drink alcohol, brewing the perfect cup of tea is a wonderful skill to possess. It allows you to indulge in the world of fancy teas, savour their flavours and reap the numerous health benefits they offer. So, take a moment, slow down and sip on a cup of perfectly brewed tea – your taste buds and your body will thank you.

Water Temperature and Steeping Times

In the world of tea, water temperature and steeping times play a crucial role in creating the perfect cup of tea. Whether you are a tea lover, a parent looking for healthier drink choices for your kids or someone who prefers non-alcoholic beverages, understanding these factors is essential to crafting delightful and flavourful tea cocktails.

When it comes to water temperature, specific teas require different levels of heat to bring out their unique flavours. For loose-leaf teas, such as delicate white teas or green teas, it is crucial to use water that is heated below boiling point. The ideal temperature is around 175°F or 80°C, as boiling water can scorch the leaves and overpower their delicate flavours. On the other hand, black teas and herbal infusions can tolerate higher temperatures, usually around 200°F or 93°C.

Steeping times also vary depending on the type of tea you are using. Steeping is the process of soaking the tea leaves in hot water to extract their flavours and aromas. For fancy teas, shorter steeping times are recommended to avoid bitterness. Green teas typically require only 1 to 2 minutes, while white teas can be steeped for 2 to 3 minutes.

However, black teas and herbal infusions can withstand longer steeping times, usually ranging from 3 to 5 minutes, to fully develop their rich flavours.

It's important to note that steeping times can be adjusted according to personal preference. If you prefer a stronger cup of tea, you can extend the steeping time slightly, but be cautious not to exceed the recommended time to prevent bitterness.

To ensure the best results, it is advisable to use an electric kettle with temperature control or a thermometer to measure the water temperature accurately. This will help you achieve the perfect balance between flavour extraction and avoiding any unpleasant tastes.

By understanding the significance of water temperature and steeping times, you can create exquisite tea cocktails that are both refreshing and bursting with flavour. Whether you are hosting a tea party or simply enjoying a quiet evening at home, mastering these techniques will elevate your tea experience to new heights.

Fancy Tea: A Guide to Non-Alcoholic Tea Cocktails is a must-have book for tea lovers, parents seeking healthier drink choices for their kids and anyone looking to explore the world of fancy teas. With expert guidance on water temperature and steeping times, you can indulge in delicious and sophisticated tea cocktails that will impress even the most discerning palates.

Tea Brewing Tools and Techniques

In the enchanting world of tea, brewing the perfect cup requires more than just selecting the finest leaves. It is an art that involves using the right tools and techniques to unlock the full flavours and aromas of this beloved beverage. Whether you are a seasoned tea lover or someone exploring healthier drink choices, understanding tea brewing tools and techniques can elevate your tea-drinking experience to new heights.

Fancy Tea: A Guide to Non-Alcoholic Tea Cocktails

Tea brewing starts with the essential tools. A tea kettle is a must-have, allowing you to heat water to the ideal temperature for different types of tea. For a more precise approach, an electric kettle with temperature control is highly recommended. Additionally, a quality tea infuser or strainer ensures a smooth and debris-free brew. Tea enthusiasts may also enjoy the elegance of a traditional tea set, complete with a teapot, cups and saucers, adding a touch of sophistication to your tea rituals.

Now that you have the necessary tools, let's delve into the techniques that will help you brew a delightful cup of tea. The first step is understanding water temperature. Different types of tea require specific temperatures to bring out their unique flavours. Delicate green teas, for example, thrive at lower temperatures around 160 to 180°F, while robust black teas prefer hotter water around 205 to 212°F. Experimenting with water temperatures will allow you to discover your personal preferences.

The next technique to master is steeping time. The time you allow the tea leaves to infuse in hot water directly impacts the flavour of your brew. Lighter teas such as white or green teas generally require a shorter steeping time of 1 to 3 minutes, while black and herbal teas benefit from 3 to 5 minutes. Remember that over steeping can lead to bitterness, so be mindful of the recommended steeping times for each tea variety.

Lastly, don't forget to savour your tea. Take the time to appreciate the aroma and colour of your brew before indulging in its flavours. Tea drinking can be a mindful experience, allowing you to unwind and recharge. It is a versatile beverage that can be enjoyed hot or cold, and even as a base for non-alcoholic tea cocktails. The possibilities are endless, and as you explore the world of fancy tea, you'll uncover new flavours, blends and pairings that will excite your taste buds.

Whether you are a tea lover seeking to expand your knowledge or a parent looking for healthier drink choices for your kids, mastering the art of tea brewing tools and techniques is a rewarding journey. It opens up a world of flavours, aromas and experiences that will leave you enchanted, sip after sip. So grab your favourite tea, prepare your brewing tools and embark on a delightful tea adventure.

03

Chapter 3: Tea Cocktails

The Art of Mixology

Welcome to the enchanting world of mixology, where the delicate flavours of tea merge with creative ingredients to craft exquisite, non-alcoholic tea cocktails. In this subchapter, we will delve into the art of mixology, exploring the techniques, ingredients and secrets behind the creation of loose-leaf tea beverages that are sure to delight tea lovers, parents, kids and anyone seeking healthier drink choices.

Mixology is not just about combining ingredients; it is an art form that requires precision, creativity and a deep understanding of flavours. In the realm of non-alcoholic tea cocktails, the possibilities are endless. From vibrant herbal infusions to robust black teas and delicate white teas, each variety brings its unique character to the concoction.

To master the art of mixology, one must start with the fundamentals. We will explore the importance of properly brewing a tea, understanding the ideal water temperature, steeping times and the right amount of tea leaves to achieve the perfect balance of flavours. We will also uncover various brewing methods, such as cold brewing, which brings out a different dimension in taste.

Once you have mastered the brewing techniques, it's time to experiment with flavours. Add a touch of sweetness with natural sweeteners like honey or agave syrup or enhance the aroma with a hint of lavender or rose petals. Explore the world of fruits, herbs and spices, and discover their harmonious pairings with different tea varieties.

Presentation is another crucial aspect of mixology. We will guide you through the art of garnishing, using fresh herbs, edible flowers or even dried fruit slices to add a visually stunning element to your tea cocktail. Remember, the visual appeal is just as important as the taste, especially when crafting loose-leaf tea beverages.

Whether you are hosting a tea party, looking for a refreshing alternative to alcoholic drinks or simply seeking a healthier beverage choice, the art of mixology opens up a whole new world of possibilities.

Join us on this journey as we explore tantalizing recipes, share expert tips and unlock the secrets behind crafting non-alcoholic tea cocktails that will truly make you savour every sip.

So, grab your teapot, your favourite tea leaves and let your imagination run wild. The art of mixology awaits, ready to elevate your tea experience to new heights of flavour and sophistication. Cheers to healthier and more exciting tea adventures!

Essential Ingredients for Tea Cocktails

Tea lovers, parents, kids, people who don't drink alcohol and those seeking healthier drink choices will be thrilled to discover the world of non-alcoholic tea cocktails. In this subchapter, we will explore the essential ingredients that make these fancy tea concoctions truly remarkable.

1. Quality Tea: The foundation of any tea cocktail lies in the selection of high-quality tea. Whether it's black, green, herbal or white tea, ensure you choose loose-leaf tea or tea bags made from whole leaves. This guarantees a robust flavour profile and allows the tea to shine in your cocktail.

2. Fresh Fruits and Juices: Adding fresh fruits or juices to your tea cocktails not only enhances the flavour but also provides essential vitamins and minerals. Experiment with citrus fruits like lemons, limes, oranges or berries such as strawberries, raspberries or blueberries. These natural ingredients will add a refreshing twist to your drink.

3. Sweeteners: To balance the flavours, sweeteners become an important element. Opt for natural sweeteners like honey, agave nectar or maple syrup instead of refined sugar. These alternatives add a touch of sweetness without overpowering the delicate flavours of the tea.

4. Herbs and Spices: Elevate your tea cocktail game by incorporating herbs and spices. Mint leaves, basil, rosemary or even lavender can impart a delightful aroma and taste. Additionally, spices like cinnamon, ginger, cardamom or nutmeg will infuse warmth and depth into your drink.

5. Bitters and Tinctures: For those who enjoy complex flavours, bitters and tinctures are a must-have. These concentrated extracts made from herbs, roots or fruits can provide a unique twist to your tea cocktail. Experiment with flavours like orange, lavender or chamomile to create a truly memorable drink.

6. Sparkling Water or Tonic: Adding a splash of sparkling water or tonic to your tea cocktail can give it a delightful effervescence. This addition not only enhances the visual appeal but also adds a refreshing touch to the overall experience.

Remember, the art of creating non-alcoholic tea cocktails lies in the balance of flavours and the quality of ingredients. By exploring and experimenting with these essential components, you can create a wide range of fancy tea cocktails that will delight your palate and impress your guests.

So, go ahead and start your journey into the world of non-alcoholic tea cocktails, where health, taste and sophistication come together in perfect harmony. Sip, savour and enjoy!

Tools for Tea Cocktail Making

When it comes to creating delightful and refreshing tea cocktails, having the right tools at your disposal can make all the difference. These tools not only enhance the aesthetic appeal of your drink but also help infuse the flavours in a way that elevates your tea cocktail experience. Whether you are a tea lover, a parent looking for healthier drink choices for your kids or someone who doesn't drink alcohol, this subchapter will guide you through the essential tools for mastering the art of fancy tea cocktail making.

1. Tea Infuser:
A tea infuser is an indispensable tool for steeping loose tea leaves. It allows you to extract the full flavour of the tea without any mess. Invest in a high-quality infuser that can be easily opened and cleaned, ensuring that none of the tea leaves escape into your drink.

2. Tea Strainer:
For those who prefer using tea bags, a tea strainer is a must-have. This tool helps filter out any stray tea leaves or particles, ensuring a smooth and enjoyable drinking experience.

3. Muddler:

To extract the flavours from fresh ingredients like fruits, herbs or spices, a muddler is essential. This tool allows you to gently crush and release the aromas, creating a harmonious blend of flavours in your tea cocktail.

4. Cocktail Shaker:

A cocktail shaker is a versatile tool that enables you to mix your tea cocktails with precision. It ensures that all the ingredients are thoroughly combined, creating a well-balanced and refreshing drink. Look for a shaker with a built-in strainer for added convenience.

5. Jigger:

When it comes to creating the perfect tea cocktail, precise measurements are vital. A jigger, a small measuring tool with two sides of different capacities, allows you to accurately measure the ingredients and maintain consistency in your drinks.

6. Glassware:

To truly embrace the fancy tea experience, investing in elegant glassware is highly recommended. Opt for tall, slender glasses that showcase the vibrant colours and layers of your tea cocktails. The aesthetic appeal of the glassware enhances the overall enjoyment of your drink.

By equipping yourself with these essential tools, you will be well-prepared to embark on a journey of tea cocktail making. Whether you are a tea lover, a health-conscious individual or a parent seeking healthier alternatives for your children, these tools will help you create delicious and visually appealing drinks that are sure to impress. So, grab your favourite tea, gather your tools and let your creativity flow as you dive into the world of non-alcoholic tea cocktails. Cheers to a healthier and a more enjoyable drinking experience!

Fancy Tea: A Guide to Non-Alcoholic Tea Cocktails

Proper Glassware for Serving

When it comes to enjoying a delightful tea cocktail or a refreshing non-alcoholic beverage, the choice of glassware can enhance the overall experience. The right glass can elevate the presentation, aroma and taste of your drink. In this subchapter, we will explore the various types of glassware that are perfect for serving your fancy tea creations.

Teacups: Teacups are a timeless classic and are ideal for serving traditional teas. The delicate and elegant design of teacups allows the aromas to be fully appreciated. For those who prefer a more formal experience, teacups with saucers can add a touch of sophistication to your tea-serving ritual. Teacups come in various sizes and shapes, so be sure to choose one that suits your personal style.

Mugs: For a more casual and cozy tea-drinking experience, mugs are the way to go. They are perfect for those who prefer a larger serving size or love to snuggle up with a warm cup of tea. Mugs can come in a wide range of designs and materials, from classic ceramic to modern glass or stainless steel. Find a mug that not only reflects your personality but also keeps your tea at the perfect sipping temperature.

Double-walled glasses: If you enjoy iced teas or want to create visually stunning layered tea cocktails, double-walled glasses are a must-have. These glasses have two walls that provide insulation, keeping your drink cool while preventing condensation from forming on the exterior. The transparency of the glass allows you to appreciate the beautiful colour gradients of layered drinks, making them a stylish addition to any tea lover's collection.

Tumblers: Tumblers are versatile and practical glassware options, suitable for both hot and cold tea beverages. They are often designed with lids and straws, making them ideal for on-the-go tea enthusiasts or parents who want spill-proof options for their kids. Tumblers come in various sizes, so you can choose one that perfectly accommodates your preferred tea serving size.

Regardless of the glassware you choose, always remember to handle it with care. Avoid extreme temperature changes and ensure proper cleaning to preserve the quality and longevity of your glassware.

By selecting the right glassware for serving your fancy tea creations, you can elevate your tea-drinking experience to new heights. Whether you are a tea lover, a parent looking for healthier drink choices for your kids or someone who does not consume alcohol, investing in proper glassware will enhance the visual appeal and enjoyment of your non-alcoholic tea cocktails. So, take a moment to sip, savour and appreciate the beauty and taste of your favourite teas in the perfect glassware.

04

Chapter 4: Classic Non-Alcoholic Tea Cocktails

Early Grey Sunrise recipe

Subchapter: Earl Grey Sunrise

Welcome to the delightful world of non-alcoholic tea cocktails! In this subchapter, we will explore the intriguing and sophisticated drink known as the Earl Grey Sunrise. Perfect for tea lovers, parents, kids and anyone seeking healthier drink choices, this fancy tea cocktail is sure to captivate your taste buds and provide a refreshing experience.

The Earl Grey Sunrise is a unique twist on the classic Sunrise cocktail, replacing the traditional alcoholic ingredients with the elegance and complexity of Earl Grey tea. This delicious concoction harmoniously combines the vibrant flavours of citrus and floral notes found in Earl Grey, creating a drink that is both uplifting and rejuvenating.

To craft the Earl Grey Sunrise, start by steeping a high-quality Earl Grey tea in hot water. Allow the tea to infuse for a few minutes, ensuring the full extraction of its aromatic flavours. Once brewed, let it cool down to room temperature.

Next, fill a tall glass with ice cubes and pour the chilled Earl Grey tea over it. As the tea cascades over the ice, it releases its mesmerizing aroma, creating a sensory experience that is both visually appealing and enticing. Watch as the dark amber hue of the tea intertwines with the glistening ice, resembling a captivating sunrise.

To enhance the flavour profile of the Earl Grey Sunrise, add a splash of freshly squeezed orange juice. The citrusy tang of the juice complements the floral undertones of the tea, creating a harmonious and well-balanced blend. For an extra touch of sweetness, you can drizzle a bit of honey or agave syrup into the mix.

Garnish your creation with a thin slice of orange or a sprig of fresh lavender, allowing the drink to showcase its sophistication and elegance. Take a moment to appreciate the vibrant colours and enticing aroma that emanate from your glass.

The Earl Grey Sunrise is not just a delightful drink but also a healthier alternative to traditional cocktails. It offers all the pleasure and indulgence of a fancy tea cocktail, without the negative effects of alcohol. Whether you're a tea enthusiast, a parent looking for a special treat for your kids or simply someone exploring healthier drink choices, the Earl Grey Sunrise is sure to become a favourite in your repertoire.

Embrace the art of tea mixology and savour the exquisite flavours of the Earl Grey Sunrise. Cheers to a refreshing and captivating journey through the world of non-alcoholic tea cocktails!

Subchapter: Matcha Mojito: A Refreshing Twist on a Classic

Introduction:
In the world of loose-leaf tea, where unique flavours and elegant presentations are celebrated, the Matcha Mojito stands out as a refreshing and health-conscious choice. This delightful concoction combines the vibrant flavours of matcha, the traditional Japanese powdered green tea, with the invigorating elements of a classic mojito. Perfect for tea lovers, parents and anyone seeking healthier drink options, the Matcha Mojito offers a delightful burst of flavour without the need for alcohol.

The Matcha Mojito Recipe

Ingredients:
- 1 teaspoon of matcha powder
- 1 tablespoon of fresh lime juice
- 1 tablespoon of agave syrup (or sweetener of your choice)
- 6 8 fresh mint leaves
- Club soda or sparkling water
- Ice cubes

Instructions:
1. In a tall glass, muddle the mint leaves gently to release their aromatic oils.
2. Add the matcha powder, lime juice, and agave syrup to the glass.
3. Fill the glass halfway with ice cubes and stir the mixture well.
4. Top off the glass with club soda or sparkling water, and give it a final stir.
5. Garnish with a sprig of fresh mint and a lime wedge.
6. Serve immediately and enjoy the refreshing flavours of the Matcha Mojito.

The Health Benefits:
As a non-alcoholic tea cocktail, the Matcha Mojito offers numerous health benefits that make it an ideal choice for those seeking a healthier drink option. Matcha is rich in antioxidants, which help combat free radicals in the body and promote overall well-being. It also provides a gentle energy boost without the jitters often associated with caffeine. Additionally, the use of fresh lime juice and mint leaves adds a refreshing twist while providing a dose of essential vitamins and minerals.

Conclusion
The Matcha Mojito is a wonderful addition to your repertoire of fancy tea recipes. Its vibrant green colour, invigorating flavours and health-conscious ingredients make it a perfect choice for tea lovers, parents and individuals looking for non-alcoholic, healthier drink choices. Whether you're hosting a tea party, spending quality time with your kids or simply craving a fresh and revitalizing beverage, the Matcha Mojito is sure to impress with its unique fusion of matcha and classic mojito elements. So, sip, savour and enjoy this delightful tea cocktail that combines elegance, flavour and health in every refreshing sip.

Hibiscus Margarita

Hibiscus Margarita: A Refreshing Twist on a Classic Mocktail

For tea lovers, parents, kids and anyone seeking healthier drink alternatives, the world of loose-leaf tea offers a delightful array of flavours and possibilities. In our book, 'Fancy Tea: A Guide to Non-Alcoholic Tea Cocktails', we aim to introduce you to the art of crafting exquisite and refreshing mocktails. One such enchanting creation is the Hibiscus Margarita, a vibrant twist on the classic cocktail that will dazzle your taste buds and leave you longing for more.

The Hibiscus Margarita is a perfect choice for those seeking a non-alcoholic beverage bursting with flavour and health benefits. Hibiscus tea is known for its stunning ruby red colour and tart, tangy taste. It is packed with antioxidants and vitamins, making it a wonderful addition to any wellness routine. By blending the exotic allure of hibiscus tea with the zesty zest of citrus flavours, we have created a mocktail that will transport you to a tropical paradise with every sip.

To prepare the Hibiscus Margarita, start by steeping a generous amount of hibiscus tea in boiling water until it reaches a deep and vibrant hue. Allow it to cool before adding freshly squeezed lime juice, a touch of agave syrup for sweetness and a splash of sparkling water for some effervescence. Stir gently and serve over ice, garnishing with a slice of lime or a sprig of fresh mint for an added touch of elegance.

The result is a visually stunning mocktail that dances on your palate, with the tangy hibiscus and lime flavours harmonizing perfectly. The natural sweetness from the agave syrup complements the tartness, creating a well-balanced and refreshing drink that is suitable for all ages and occasions. Whether you're hosting a dinner party, enjoying a family gathering or simply unwinding after a long day, the Hibiscus Margarita is a delightful choice.

So, raise your glass and join us in celebrating the endless possibilities of loose-leaf tea. With its vibrant colour, invigorating flavours and numerous health benefits, the Hibiscus Margarita is a testament to the magic that can be created when tea takes centre stage in the world of mocktails. Cheers to a healthier and more flavourful alternative for all those seeking to sip and savour life's little pleasures!

Purple Island (with blue pea butterfly and lemon)

Welcome to the enchanting world of Purple Island, where a mesmerizing blend of colours and flavours awaits you. In this subchapter, we will explore a delightful tea cocktail that combines the vibrant hues of blue pea butterfly and the tangy zest of lemon. Perfect for both tea lovers and those seeking healthier drink choices, the Purple Island cocktail is a must-try for anyone who appreciates the art of loose-leaf tea.

Let's dive into the magical ingredients that make this drink so special. The star of the show is the blue pea butterfly flower, also known as Clitoria ternatea. Renowned for its stunning blue petals, this flower not only adds a breathtaking visual element to your tea but also offers numerous health benefits. Packed with antioxidants, blue pea butterfly tea is believed to improve brain function, reduce anxiety and promote healthy skin.

To create the Purple Island cocktail, start by brewing a cup of blue pea butterfly tea. As the water infuses with the petals, a mesmerizing transformation takes place, turning the liquid into a deep indigo hue. Once the tea has steeped to perfection, add a squeeze of fresh lemon juice. The citrusy notes of lemon beautifully complement the floral undertones of the blue pea butterfly, creating a balanced and refreshing flavour profile.

This vibrant tea cocktail is not only a treat for the taste buds but also a visual delight. The combination of rich purple and vibrant yellow from the lemon creates a stunning colour palette that is sure to impress both kids and adults alike. Parents can introduce this exciting beverage to their little ones, offering a healthier alternative to sugary drinks.

Whether you're hosting a fancy tea party or simply craving a unique and invigorating drink, the Purple Island cocktail is a delightful choice. Its alluring colours, refreshing flavours and health benefits make it a perfect choice for tea enthusiasts and those seeking non-alcoholic options. So, why not transport yourself to the captivating Purple Island and experience the wonders of this magical tea cocktail? Sip and savour the beauty of nature in a cup, one sip at a time.

Jasmine Lemonade

Jasmine Lemonade: A Refreshing Twist on a Classic Favourite

In the world of fancy tea, where elegance and sophistication meet in a delicate balance, there is one drink that stands out – Jasmine Lemonade. This delightful concoction combines the fragrant notes of jasmine flowers with the tangy freshness of lemons, creating a drink that is both invigorating and soothing to the senses.

For tea lovers, Jasmine Lemonade offers a unique experience that goes beyond the traditional cup of tea. It is a delicious alternative that allows you to indulge in the flavours of tea while quenching your thirst on a hot summer day. The delicate aroma of jasmine takes centre stage, infusing every sip with a floral sweetness that is simply enchanting.

Parents searching for healthier drink choices for their kids will be delighted to discover Jasmine Lemonade. It is a non-alcoholic option that not only provides hydration but also introduces children to the world of tea in a fun and approachable way. With its vibrant yellow hue and irresistible fragrance, it is sure to capture their attention and encourage them to explore new flavours.

For those who don't drink alcohol or prefer non-alcoholic alternatives, Jasmine Lemonade is a perfect choice. It offers a sophisticated beverage option that can be enjoyed at social gatherings or as a relaxing treat at home. Its light and refreshing nature make it an ideal companion for those looking to unwind and savour the moment without the effects of alcohol.

In addition to its remarkable taste, Jasmine Lemonade also boasts several health benefits. Jasmine tea is known for its calming properties, helping to reduce stress and anxiety. The addition of fresh lemons provides a dose of vitamin C, boosting the immune system and promoting overall well-being. It is a guilt-free indulgence that nourishes both the body and the soul.

Whether you are a tea lover, a parent seeking healthier options or someone looking for a loose-leaf tea alternative, Jasmine Lemonade is a delightful choice. Its delicate blend of flavours and elegant presentation make it a standout in the world of non-alcoholic tea cocktails. So, pour yourself a glass, sit back and let the enchanting aroma of jasmine transport you to a state of pure bliss. Cheers to a refreshing and healthier choice!

Goddess Spritzer-Herbal Heaven

Subchapter: Goddess Spritzer - Herbal Heaven

Introduction:
For tea lovers, parents, kids and anyone seeking healthier drink choices, our book 'Fancy Tea: A Guide to Non-Alcoholic Tea Cocktails' brings you the exquisite world of fancy tea. In this subchapter, we present you with the delightful recipe of Goddess Spritzer - Herbal Heaven. This refreshing and invigorating blend of herbs will transport you to a heavenly realm, offering a unique and satisfying experience.

Recipe:
The Goddess Spritzer - Herbal Heaven is a divine fusion of herbs and botanicals, carefully selected to create a harmonious blend that tantalizes your taste buds. This recipe not only promises a burst of flavours but also provides numerous health benefits. Let's dive into the enchanting world of this herbal elixir.

Ingredients:
- 1 teaspoon chamomile flowers
- 1 teaspoon lavender buds
- 1 teaspoon hibiscus petals
- 1 teaspoon rose petals
- 1 teaspoon lemon balm leaves
- 1 cup filtered water
- 1 cup sparkling water
- Honey or agave nectar (optional)
- Ice cubes
- Fresh mint leaves and lemon slices for garnish

Instructions:

1. In a teapot or a heat-resistant container, combine the chamomile flowers, lavender buds, hibiscus petals, rose petals and lemon balm leaves.
2. Boil the filtered water and pour it over the herbal blend in the teapot.
3. Allow the mixture to steep for approximately 5 to 7 minutes, ensuring the flavours are fully infused.
4. Once steeped, strain the herbal infusion into a pitcher and let it cool.
5. Add the sparkling water to the pitcher and stir gently to combine.
6. Taste the spritzer and, if desired, add honey or agave nectar to sweeten.
7. Fill serving glasses with ice cubes and pour the Goddess Spritzer - Herbal Heaven over the ice.
8. Garnish each glass with fresh mint leaves and a slice of lemon for an extra burst of freshness.
9. Serve immediately and enjoy the heavenly goodness!

Conclusion:

The Goddess Spritzer - Herbal Heaven is a true masterpiece, combining the delicate flavours of chamomile, lavender, hibiscus, rose and lemon balm. This non-alcoholic tea cocktail is not only visually stunning but also a perfect choice for tea lovers, parents, kids and those looking for healthier drink options. Embark on this journey to herbal heaven, where every sip will transport you to a realm of tranquillity and pure bliss. Cheers to a world of loose-leaf tea!

This vibrant tea cocktail is not only a treat for the taste buds but also a visual delight. The combination of rich purple and vibrant yellow from the lemon creates a stunning colour palette that is sure to impress both kids and adults alike. Parents can introduce this exciting beverage to their little ones, offering a healthier alternative to sugary drinks.

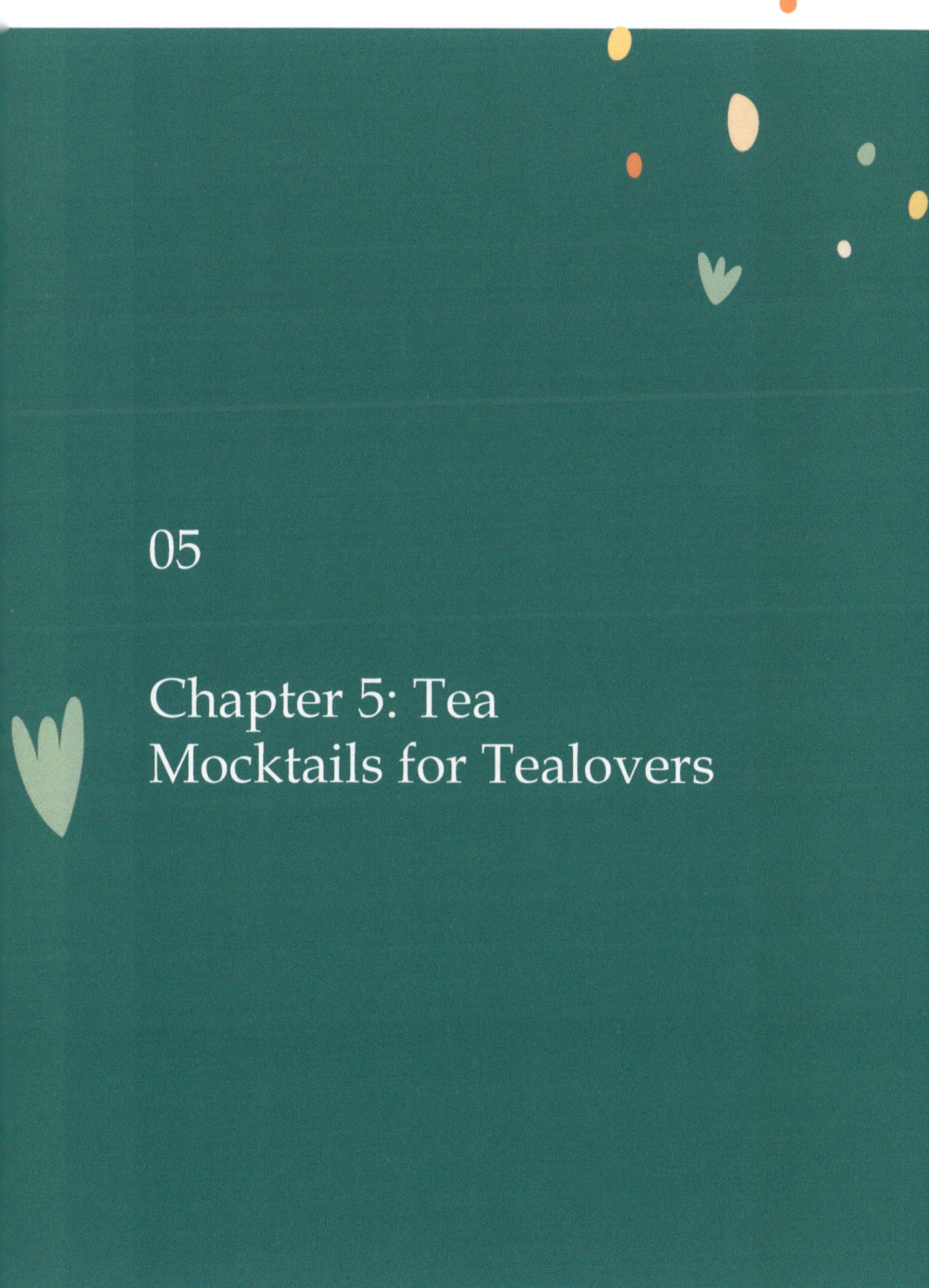

05

Chapter 5: Tea Mocktails for Tealovers

Fancy Tea: A Guide to Non-Alcoholic Tea Cocktails

Minty Iced Tea Punch

Welcome to the subchapter dedicated to the delightful Minty Iced Tea Punch! This refreshing and flavourful concoction will surely satisfy your taste buds and quench your thirst, making it the ideal beverage for tea lovers, parents, kids and anyone seeking healthier drink choices.

In the world of loose-leaf tea, this Minty Iced Tea Punch stands out as a delightful option for those who want to enjoy a non-alcoholic tea cocktail. Bursting with the vibrant flavours of mint and tea, this recipe offers a unique twist on traditional iced tea that will captivate your senses.

To begin, gather the following **ingredients:**

- 4 cups of brewed tea (green or black, depending on your preference)
- 1 cup of fresh mint leaves
- 1 cup of freshly squeezed lemon juice
- 1/2 cup of honey or your preferred sweetener

- 2 cups of sparkling water or club soda
- Ice cubes
- Lemon slices and fresh mint sprigs for garnish

Start by brewing the tea according to the package instructions. Once brewed, allow it to cool to room temperature. In the meantime, muddle the fresh mint leaves in a separate bowl to release their aromatic oils and flavours.

Once the tea has cooled, strain it into a large pitcher and add the muddled mint leaves, freshly squeezed lemon juice and honey. Stir well until the honey dissolves completely. Place the pitcher in the refrigerator for about an hour to allow the flavours to meld and the infusion of mint to intensify.

When you're ready to serve, remove the pitcher from the refrigerator and add the sparkling water or club soda to give the punch a delightful fizz. Fill glasses with ice cubes and pour the Minty Iced Tea Punch over the ice, garnishing each glass with a lemon slice and a fresh mint sprig.

This Minty Iced Tea Punch is a perfect companion for summer gatherings, picnics or simply for a relaxing afternoon at home. Its invigorating minty flavour combined with the subtle sweetness of honey and the tanginess of lemon will leave you feeling refreshed and rejuvenated.

Enjoy this delightful non-alcoholic tea cocktail and savour the goodness of a healthier, loose-leaf tea option. Cheers to your well-being and the joy of sipping on a delicious Minty Iced Tea Punch!

Lemongrass and Ginger Refresher

Lemongrass and Ginger Refresher: A Refreshing Twist for Tea Lovers

Are you a tea lover in search of a fancy beverage that is both delicious and alcohol-free? Look no further! In this subchapter, we present to you an exquisite recipe for a Lemongrass and Ginger Refresher, straight from the pages of 'Sip and Savor: A Guide to Non-Alcoholic Tea Cocktails'. This tantalizing blend is perfect for parents, kids and anyone seeking healthier drink choices.

Combining the invigorating flavours of lemongrass and ginger, this refreshing tea cocktail is not only a treat for your taste buds but also a boon for your health. Lemongrass, known for its citrusy aroma and delicate flavour, adds a zesty twist to any beverage. It

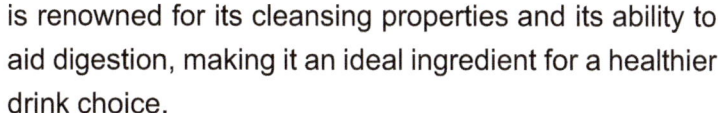

is renowned for its cleansing properties and its ability to aid digestion, making it an ideal ingredient for a healthier drink choice.

Ginger, on the other hand, brings a warm and spicy kick to this concoction. Its medicinal properties have been celebrated for centuries, known to soothe nausea, improve circulation and reduce inflammation. Together, lemongrass and ginger create a harmonious blend that will awaken your senses and leave you feeling revitalized.

To create this delightful Lemongrass and Ginger Refresher, start by brewing a strong lemongrass tea. You can find dried lemongrass in most specialty tea stores or grow your own if you have a green thumb. Once brewed, allow the tea to cool to room temperature.

Next, prepare a ginger simple syrup by simmering fresh ginger slices with sugar and water until the flavours meld together in a sweet and spicy syrup. Allow it to cool before straining out the ginger pieces.

Now it's time to bring everything together. In a glass filled with ice, pour the lemongrass tea, add a splash of ginger simple syrup and give it a gentle stir. Take a moment to inhale the enticing aroma that wafts up from the glass before taking a sip.

The Lemongrass and Ginger Refresher is not only a delightful beverage for tea enthusiasts, but it is also a perfect alternative for those seeking healthier drink choices. Its vibrant flavours and health benefits make it an ideal option for parents looking to introduce their kids to fancy tea cocktails without alcohol. So go ahead, indulge in this sensational creation and savour every sip of this unique and invigorating blend!

Tropical Tea Cooler
Tropical Tea Cooler

Welcome to the exciting world of non-alcoholic tea cocktails! In this sub-chapter, we bring you a delightful recipe that will transport your taste buds to a tropical paradise - the Tropical Tea Cooler. Perfect for tea lovers, parents, kids and anyone seeking healthier drink choices, this fancy tea concoction will surely become a favourite in your household.

Ingredients:
- 2 cups of brewed tropical fruit tea (pineapple, mango or passionfruit)
- 1 cup of pineapple juice
- 1 cup of orange juice
- 1 tablespoon of honey (optional)
- Ice cubes
- Fresh mint leaves for garnish

Instructions:

1. Start by brewing two cups of your favourite tropical fruit tea. You can choose from flavours like pineapple, mango or passionfruit, depending on your preference. Allow the tea to cool to room temperature.

2. In a large pitcher, combine the brewed tropical fruit tea, pineapple juice and orange juice. Stir gently to mix the flavours.

3. If you prefer a sweeter taste, add a tablespoon of honey to the mixture and stir until it dissolves completely. Feel free to adjust the sweetness level according to your liking.

4. Fill tall glasses with ice cubes and pour the tropical tea cooler over the ice. The refreshing combination of flavours will instantly transport you to an exotic island getaway.

5. To add a touch of elegance, garnish each glass with a sprig of fresh mint leaves. Not only does it enhance the visual appeal, but it also adds a subtle hint of freshness to the drink.

The Tropical Tea Cooler is a wonderful beverage option for both adults and children. It offers a healthier alternative to sugary sodas or artificially flavoured drinks. The natural sweetness from the tropical fruit tea and juices, along with the optional honey, makes it a guilt-free treat that can be enjoyed any time of the day.

So, whether you are hosting a tea party, looking for a refreshing drink to cool down on a hot summer day or simply want to explore the world of non-alcoholic tea cocktails, the Tropical Tea Cooler is the perfect choice.

Embrace the flavours of the tropics and indulge in this tasty, loose-leaf tea creation. Cheers to a healthier, more enjoyable beverage experience!

Spice Apple Chai Mocktail

Spiced Apple Chai Mocktail Recipe: A Delightful Blend of Flavours for Tea Lovers and Health-Conscious Individuals

For all the tea lovers, parents, kids and individuals seeking healthier drink choices, we present to you an exquisite recipe from the book 'Fancy Tea: A Guide to Non-Alcoholic Tea Cocktails' – the Spiced Apple Chai Mocktail. This fancy tea-based beverage is a heavenly fusion of aromatic spices, tangy apples and the comforting warmth of chai. Get ready to indulge in a burst of flavours without any guilt!

Ingredients:
- 2 cups of apple juice
- 1 cup of brewed chai tea (prepare according to package instructions)

- 1 cinnamon stick
- 2 cloves
- 2 cardamom pods, slightly crushed
- 1-inch piece of fresh ginger, thinly sliced
- 1 tablespoon of honey or maple syrup (optional)
- Apple slices and cinnamon powder for garnish

Instructions:

1. In a saucepan, combine the apple juice, brewed chai tea, cinnamon stick, cloves, cardamom pods and ginger. Bring the mixture to a gentle simmer over low heat.

2. Let the flavours infuse for about 10 minutes, allowing the spices to release their aromatic essence into the liquid.

3. If desired, sweeten the mocktail with honey or maple syrup. Stir well until the sweetener dissolves completely.

4. Remove the saucepan from heat and strain the liquid to remove the spices, ginger and any sediment.
This step ensures a smooth and enjoyable drinking experience.

5. Allow the spiced apple chai mocktail to cool for a few minutes before refrigerating it for at least an hour to enhance the flavours.

6. Once chilled, pour the mocktail into serving glasses filled with ice cubes.

7. Garnish each glass with a slice of apple and a sprinkle of cinnamon powder to add an elegant touch.

Serve the Spiced Apple Chai Mocktail to your guests or enjoy it with your family, relishing every sip of the delightful blend.

This mocktail recipe is perfect for those special occasions when you desire a sophisticated and healthier alternative to alcoholic beverages. It provides a fantastic opportunity for parents to bond with their children over a delectable drink, creating lasting memories. Moreover, for individuals who do not consume alcohol, this mocktail offers a chance to partake in the joy of sipping fancy and flavourful concoctions.

Embrace the richness of the Spiced Apple Chai Mocktail and raise your glass to a refreshing, health-conscious indulgence. Cheers to a world of non-alcoholic tea cocktails that cater to your taste buds, your well-being and your love for tea!

Lavender Lemon Fizz

For the tea lovers, parents, kids and anyone looking for healthier drink choices, we have a delightful recipe to share from our book

'Fancy Tea: A Guide to Non-Alcoholic Tea Cocktails'. This subchapter is dedicated to the exquisite Lavender Lemon Fizz. If you are a fan of fancy tea, get ready to indulge in this aromatic and refreshing concoction!

Ingredients:
- 2 cups of brewed lavender tea
- 1 cup of freshly squeezed lemon juice
- 1/4 cup of honey or agave syrup
- Sparkling water
- Ice cubes
- Fresh lavender sprigs (for garnish)

Instructions:

1. Start by brewing a strong cup of lavender tea. Allow it to steep for about 5 minutes, ensuring a fragrant infusion. Then, let it cool to room temperature.

2. In a pitcher, combine the brewed lavender tea with the freshly squeezed lemon juice. Stir in the honey or agave syrup until it dissolves completely. Adjust the sweetness according to your preference.

3. Fill tall glasses with ice cubes and pour the lavender lemon mixture over the ice, filling each glass about halfway.

4. Top off each glass with sparkling water, adding a refreshing effervescence to the drink. Give it a gentle stir to combine all the flavours.

5. Garnish each glass with a fresh lavender sprig, not only enhancing the visual appeal but also infusing a delicate aroma.

The Lavender Lemon Fizz is a perfect beverage for any occasion. Its light and floral notes from the lavender tea, combined with the tanginess of freshly squeezed lemon, create a harmonious balance of flavours. The addition of sparkling water adds a delightful effervescence, making it a sophisticated yet refreshing drink.

This recipe is not only ideal for adults who choose to abstain from alcohol but also a great choice for parents and kids. It provides a healthier alternative to sugary sodas and artificially flavoured drinks. Lavender is known for its calming properties, making it a perfect choice for winding down after a long day or as a soothing option for children.

So, whether you're hosting a tea party, enjoying a relaxing afternoon by yourself or looking for a way to hydrate your kids with a fancy twist, the Lavender Lemon Fizz is a must-try. Sip and savour this non-alcoholic tea cocktail, and let its delightful flavours transport you to a state of pure bliss.

Cherry Berry Iced Tea

Chapter 3 Cherry Berry Iced Tea

Welcome to the world of loose-leaf tea! In this subchapter, we will explore a delightful and refreshing recipe called Cherry Berry Iced Tea. Perfect for tea lovers, parents, kids and anyone seeking healthier drink choices, this non-alcoholic tea cocktail will surely become a favourite in your household.

Ingredients:
- 4 cups of water
- 4 teaspoons of fruit tea blend (such as cherry and berry)
- 2 tablespoons of honey or sugar (optional)
- 1 cup of cherries, pitted and halved
- 1 cup of mixed berries (strawberries, blueberries, raspberries)
- Fresh mint leaves for garnish
- Ice cubes

Instructions:

1. Boil four cups of water in a medium-sized pot. Once the water reaches a rolling boil, remove it from the heat and let it cool for a minute.

2. Add four teaspoons of your favourite fruit tea blend to the pot. Allow the tea to steep for 5 to 7 minutes, or until it reaches your desired strength. You can adjust the steeping time according to your taste preferences.

3. If you prefer a sweeter taste, add two tablespoons of honey or sugar to the tea while it's still warm. Stir until the sweetener is completely dissolved.

4. Set the tea aside to cool completely. You can speed up the process by placing it in the refrigerator for about 30 minutes.

5. Once the tea has cooled, strain it into a pitcher or a large glass jar to remove any tea leaves or fruit bits.

6. Add the pitted and halved cherries and the mixed berries to the pitcher, gently pressing them with a spoon to release their juices and flavours.

7. Place the pitcher in the refrigerator for at least an hour to allow the flavours to infuse.

8. When ready to serve, fill glasses with ice cubes and pour the chilled Cherry Berry Iced Tea over them.

9. Garnish each glass with a sprig of fresh mint leaves for a touch of elegance and aroma.

Enjoy this enchanting Cherry Berry Iced Tea as a refreshing beverage on a sunny afternoon, or serve it at your next gathering to impress your guests with its vibrant colours and enticing flavours. Cheers to a healthier and more enjoyable tea-drinking experience!

06

Chapter 6: Tea Cocktails for Parents and Kids

Fruity Tea Popsicles

Tea lovers, parents, kids and anyone looking for healthier drink choices will be delighted by this refreshing and delicious Fruity Tea Popsicles recipe. In the world of loose-leaf tea, these popsicles are a delightful twist that combines the goodness of tea with the fun and coolness of a frozen treat.

Ingredients:
- 2 cups of your favourite fruity tea (such as berry or citrus)
- 1 cup of mixed fresh fruits (berries, sliced peaches or any other fruits you enjoy)
- 1 tablespoon of honey or agave syrup (optional, for added sweetness)

Instructions:
1. Brew your fruity tea according to the instructions on the package. Allow it to cool completely before moving on to the next step.

2. Once the tea has cooled, add the mixed fresh fruits to the tea. Stir gently to combine. If you prefer a sweeter popsicle, you can add honey or agave syrup at this stage.

3. Pour the fruity tea mixture into popsicle moulds, leaving a little space at the top for expansion. If you don't have popsicle moulds, you can use small paper cups and insert popsicle sticks in the centre.

4. Place the popsicle moulds or cups in the freezer and let them set for about 1 hour. Then, insert popsicle sticks into each mould, ensuring they stand upright.

5. Return the popsicles to the freezer and let them freeze completely, usually for about 4 to 6 hours or overnight.

6. When you're ready to enjoy these delectable treats, simply run the moulds or cups under warm water for a few seconds to loosen the popsicles. Gently pull them out and savour the delightful combination of fruity tea and fresh fruits.

These Fruity Tea Popsicles are not only a tasty alternative to sugary popsicles, but they also provide a dose of antioxidants and vitamins from the tea and fresh fruits. They are perfect for tea enthusiasts who want to explore new ways of enjoying their favourite beverage, as well as parents who are looking for healthier options for their kids.

So, whether you're lounging by the pool, hosting a tea party or simply looking for a guilt-free dessert, these Fruity Tea Popsicles are sure to be a hit. Cool down, savour the flavours and indulge in a delightful treat that combines the best of loose-leaf tea and a refreshing frozen delight.

Welcome to the world of fancy tea! In this chapter, we will be exploring the enchanting Blue Magic Iced Tea, featuring the mesmerizing blue pea butterfly flower. This delightful and healthy beverage is perfect for tea lovers, parents, kids, non-alcohol drinkers and anyone seeking healthier drink choices.

Blue Magic Iced Tea is not only a feast for the eyes but also a treat for your taste buds. Let's dive into the recipe and discover the wonders of this unique tea cocktail.

Ingredients:
- 2 cups water
- 2 blue pea butterfly flowers
- 2 teaspoons honey or agave syrup (optional)
- 1 lemon, juiced
- Ice cubes
- Fresh mint leaves (for garnish)

Instructions:

1. In a small saucepan, bring the water to a boil. Once boiling, remove from heat and add the blue pea butterfly flowers. Let steep for 10 minutes to infuse the water with its stunning blue colour and delicate flavour.

2. After steeping, strain the liquid into a pitcher, discarding the flowers. If desired, add honey or agave syrup for sweetness and stir until dissolved.

3. Squeeze the juice of one lemon into the pitcher, giving the tea a tangy twist. Stir to combine all the flavours.

4. Allow the tea to cool to room temperature, and then transfer it to the refrigerator to chill for at least an hour.

5. When ready to serve, fill tall glasses with ice cubes and pour the chilled Blue Magic Iced Tea over them. The vibrant blue colour will immediately capture your attention.

6. For an added touch of elegance, garnish each glass with a sprig of fresh mint leaves. Not only does it enhance the visual appeal, but it also contributes a refreshing aroma.

Blue Magic Iced Tea offers a refreshing and healthier alternative to sugary drinks. The blue pea butterfly flowers are not only visually stunning but also rich in antioxidants, which promote overall well-being. This beverage is perfect for sipping on hot summer days, hosting a fancy tea party or even as a delightful treat for children.

So, grab your favourite tea set, invite your friends and family and prepare to be mesmerized by the enchanting Blue Magic Iced Tea. Sip, savour and indulge in this delightful concoction that will leave everyone enchanted and craving for more. Enjoy!

Tea-infused Smoothies

Tea-infused Smoothies: A Healthy and Flavourful Twist for Tea Lovers, Parents and Health Enthusiasts

Introduction:
Tea lovers, parents and health-conscious individuals are constantly seeking new and exciting ways to enjoy their favourite beverages. In the world of loose-leaf tea, where creativity knows no bounds, tea-infused smoothies have emerged as a delightful and nutritious choice. This subchapter explores various tea-infused smoothie recipes that will elevate your tea-drinking experience to new heights. Whether you're looking for a refreshing drink for yourself or a healthier option for your kids, these smoothies are sure to tantalize your taste buds and provide a burst of energy and wellness.

1. The Green Goddess Smoothie:
This vibrant smoothie combines the goodness of green tea with a medley of fresh fruits and leafy greens. Packed with antioxidants, vitamins and minerals, it's an ideal drink to kickstart your day or revitalize your energy levels. The recipe includes a blend of matcha green tea, spinach, mango, banana and a touch of honey for a naturally sweet taste.

Fancy Tea: A Guide to Non-Alcoholic Tea Cocktails

2. Berry-licious Chai Delight:
For those who crave the rich and aromatic flavours of chai tea, this smoothie is a dream come true. By infusing a strong black tea base with cinnamon, cardamom and cloves, we create a chai concentrate that forms the heart of this recipe. Mixed with a variety of mixed berries, almond milk and a hint of maple syrup, this smoothie is a delightful treat for kids and adults alike.

3. Tropical Paradise Infusion:
Escape to a tropical paradise with this exotic tea-infused smoothie. Blending the essence of hibiscus tea, pineapple, coconut milk and a squeeze of lime, this refreshing concoction transports you to a sunny beach with each sip. Perfect for a summer afternoon or a brunch gathering, this smoothie will leave you feeling rejuvenated and satisfied.

Conclusion:

Tea-infused smoothies offer a delightful alternative to traditional tea drinking, infusing your favourite brews with an array of flavours and nutritional benefits. Whether you're a tea enthusiast, a parent seeking healthier drink options for your kids or someone who simply wishes to explore the world of loose-leaf tea, these recipes provide a perfect starting point. Sip on these refreshing creations and savour the goodness of tea in a whole new way. Embrace the creativity, wellness and deliciousness that tea-infused smoothies bring to your life. Cheers to a world of flavourful possibilities!

Sparkling Tea Floats

If you're a tea lover, a parent looking for healthier drink options for your kids or someone who doesn't drink alcohol, this recipe is for you. In the world of fancy tea, there's a delightful and refreshing concoction that will tickle your taste buds and keep you cool on hot summer days - Sparkling Tea Floats! This whimsical and delicious recipe is perfect for tea enthusiasts who want to elevate their tea-drinking experience.

Ingredients:
- 2 cups of your favourite brewed tea (green, black or herbal)
- 1 cup sparkling water
- 1 scoop of your preferred ice cream (vanilla, chocolate or fruit-based)

Instructions:

1. Start by brewing a strong cup of your favourite tea. You can choose from green tea for its earthy flavour, black tea for a robust taste or herbal tea for a fruity and aromatic experience. Allow the tea to cool completely before proceeding.

2. Once the tea has cooled, pour it into a glass and add the sparkling water. The effervescence of the sparkling water will add a delightful fizz to your float, making it even more refreshing.

3. Gently place a scoop of your preferred ice cream on top of the tea and sparkling water mixture. Vanilla ice cream complements most tea flavours, while chocolate ice cream adds a touch of indulgence. For a fruity twist, try using a fruit-based ice cream like strawberry or mango.

4. As the ice cream melts, it will infuse the tea with its creamy goodness, creating a harmonious blend of flavours. Take a moment to indulge in the delightful combination of the tea's subtle notes and the creamy sweetness of the ice cream. Stir gently if desired.

5. Once everything is mixed to your liking, grab a spoon and straw and sip and savour every delicious mouthful of your Sparkling Tea Float. The combination of the fizzy bubbles, chilled tea and creamy ice cream will transport you to a place of pure enjoyment and refreshment.

Whether you're hosting a tea party, enjoying a lazy afternoon or simply seeking a healthier alternative to alcoholic cocktails, Sparkling Tea Floats are the perfect choice. They provide all the elegance and sophistication of fancy tea, with a playful twist that everyone can enjoy. So, gather your loved ones, prepare a batch of these delightful floats and let the magic of tea take you on a refreshing journey. Cheers to a healthier and tastier way to sip and savour!

Tea-based Slushies

Tea-based Slushies: A Refreshing Twist for All Tea Lovers

Are you a tea lover seeking a new and exciting way to enjoy your favourite beverage? Look no further! Introducing the Tea-based Slushies recipe, a delightful concoction that will tantalize your taste buds and keep you cool during the scorching summer months. This recipe is perfect for everyone, including parents, kids, those who don't drink alcohol and individuals who are looking for healthier drink choices. It's time to elevate your tea experience with a touch of fancy!

Ingredients:
- 2 cups brewed tea (choose your favourite, such as green tea, herbal tea or black tea)
- 1 cup ice cubes
- 1 tablespoon honey or maple syrup (optional, for added sweetness)
- Fresh fruit slices or mint leaves (for garnish)

Instructions:
1. Start by brewing your favourite tea. Allow it to cool to room temperature before proceeding.
2. Once the tea has cooled, pour it into a blender along with the ice cubes. If you prefer a sweeter slushie, add honey or maple syrup.
3. Blend the mixture until smooth and slushy. If needed, add more ice cubes to achieve the desired consistency.
4. Pour the tea-based slushies into serving glasses, leaving a little space at the top for garnishes.
5. To add a touch of elegance, garnish each glass with a slice of fresh fruit or a sprig of mint. This not only enhances the visual appeal but also adds a burst of flavour to your slushie.
6. Serve immediately and enjoy the refreshing taste of your Tea-based Slushies.

These slushies offer a unique twist to your regular tea routine. They are not only delicious but also packed with the health benefits that tea provides. Whether you're sipping on a green tea slushie loaded with antioxidants or indulging in a fruity herbal tea slushie, you can be confident that you're making a healthier choice compared to sugary sodas or artificially flavoured drinks.

Tea-based Slushies are perfect for family gatherings, kid-friendly parties or simply as a delightful treat for yourself. They offer a fantastic alternative to alcoholic cocktails, ensuring that everyone can partake in the celebration without compromising their preferences or health.

So, raise your glasses and toast to the art of loose-leaf tea with our Tea-based Slushies recipe. Embrace the cool, refreshing flavours and the countless possibilities that await you in the world of non-alcoholic tea cocktails. Sip and savour the goodness, knowing that you've made a choice that not only tastes great but also nourishes your body and soul.

Tea Milkshakes

Tea Milkshakes: A Delicious Twist for Tea Lovers

Indulge in the delightful fusion of two beloved beverages with these tantalizing tea milkshake recipes.

Perfect for tea lovers, parents, kids and anyone seeking healthier drink choices, these loose-leaf tea milkshakes offer a refreshing and nourishing twist to your regular tea experience. In this subchapter of 'Fancy Tea: A Guide to Non-Alcoholic Tea Cocktails', we bring you a selection of delectable recipes that will leave you craving for more.

1. Matcha Madness Milkshake:
For all the matcha enthusiasts out there, this milkshake is a true delight. Blend a scoop of vanilla ice cream, a teaspoon of matcha powder and a cup of milk until smooth and creamy. Top it off with a dollop of whipped cream and a sprinkle of matcha powder for a visually stunning masterpiece.

2. Chai Chocolate Fusion:
Indulge in the aromatic blend of chai and chocolate with this irresistible milkshake. Brew a cup of your favourite chai tea, let it cool and then blend it with a scoop of chocolate ice cream and a splash of milk. For an extra touch of decadence, garnish with a drizzle of chocolate syrup and a sprinkle of cinnamon.

3. Berry Blast Tea Shake:
For a burst of fruity flavours, this berry-infused milkshake is a must-try. Blend a handful of mixed berries, a cup of brewed fruit tea (such as hibiscus or berry blend) and a scoop of vanilla ice cream until smooth. Serve with a few fresh berries on top for a delightful visual appeal.

Fancy Tea: A Guide to Non-Alcoholic Tea Cocktails

4. Earl Grey Dream Shake:
Indulge in the elegant notes of bergamot with this sophisticated milkshake. Brew a cup of Earl Grey tea, let it cool and then blend it with a scoop of lavender-infused ice cream and a splash of milk. Garnish with a sprig of fresh lavender for an added touch of elegance.

These tea milkshakes are not only delicious but also packed with antioxidants and essential nutrients, making them a healthier alternative to traditional milkshakes. They are perfect for a hot summer day, a cozy evening treat or even a dessert option for your next gathering.

So, whether you are a tea lover, a parent looking for healthier drink choices for your kids or someone who doesn't drink alcohol, these tea milkshakes will surely satisfy your cravings and leave you wanting more. Get ready to sip and savour the exquisite flavours of these fancy tea milkshakes!

07

Chapter 7: Exploring Unique Tea Flavours

Rose-infused Tea Cocktails

For tea lovers, parents, kids, people who don't drink alcohol and those seeking healthier drink choices, we present an exquisite subchapter from our book, 'Fancy Tea: A Guide to Non-Alcoholic Tea Cocktails'. This section is dedicated to the art of Fancy Tea, with a focus on the delightful flavours of rose-infused tea cocktails.

Indulge your senses with these elegant and refreshing drinks that combine the fragrant essence of roses with the sophistication of tea. These recipes are perfect for any occasion, whether you're hosting a tea party, celebrating a special event or simply looking to elevate your daily tea routine.

1. Rose-Lemon Spritzer:
This sparkling concoction combines the zesty freshness of lemons with the delicate floral notes of rose-infused tea. Garnished with a sprig of mint and a few rose petals, this vibrant drink is a treat for the eyes and taste buds. It's a wonderful choice for kids and adults alike.

2. Rose-Infused Iced Tea:

Perfect for hot summer days, this chilled beverage is a delightful blend of rose-infused tea, honey and a splash of lemon juice. Serve it over ice, garnished with lemon slices and rose petals, for a visually stunning and refreshing drink that will keep you cool and hydrated.

3. Rose Chai Mocktail:

For those seeking a more complex flavour profile, this intriguing combination of rose-infused black tea and aromatic spices is sure to satisfy. Sweetened with a touch of honey and garnished with cinnamon sticks, this mocktail is a cozy and comforting choice for tea lovers.

4. Raspberry Rose Mock-jito:

A playful twist on the classic mojito, this mocktail features the vibrant flavours of raspberries and rose-infused tea, muddled together with lime and fresh mint leaves. Topped with sparkling water and garnished with a raspberry, this mock-jito is a crowd-pleaser that will leave everyone craving for more.

These rose-infused tea cocktails are not only delicious but also offer numerous health benefits. Roses are rich in antioxidants and known to boost the immune system and promote healthy skin. Tea, on the other hand, provides a natural source of hydration and is packed with antioxidants, vitamins and minerals.

So, embrace the world of loose-leaf tea with these exquisite rose-infused tea cocktails. Whether you're a tea lover, a parent or someone looking for healthier drink choices, these recipes will elevate your tea experience and leave you feeling refreshed, rejuvenated and satisfied. Cheers to the beauty of tea!

Ginger and Turmeric Tea Blends

For all the tea lovers out there who are looking for a healthier alternative to alcoholic cocktails, we have the perfect recipe for you. In this subchapter, we will dive into the world of fancy tea and introduce you to the delightful combination of ginger and turmeric. These two powerful ingredients not only create a flavour explosion but also offer numerous health benefits.

Ginger, known for its warm and spicy taste, has long been used in traditional medicine to aid digestion, reduce inflammation and boost the immune system. Turmeric, on the other hand, brings a vibrant golden colour to your tea, along with its anti-inflammatory and antioxidant properties. By combining these two superfoods, you can create a delightful tea blend that is not only delicious but also good for your body.

To make your very own Ginger and Turmeric Tea Blend, gather the following

- 1 tablespoon of freshly grated ginger
- 1 teaspoon of ground turmeric
- 2 cups of water

- 1 tablespoon of honey (optional, for added sweetness)
- A squeeze of fresh lemon juice (optional, for a tangy twist)

Start by bringing the water to a boil in a saucepan. Once the water is boiling, add the grated ginger and ground turmeric. Reduce the heat and let the mixture simmer for about 10 minutes, allowing the flavours to infuse into the water.

After simmering, strain the tea into your favourite teapot or individual cups. If desired, add a tablespoon of honey to sweeten the tea and a squeeze of fresh lemon juice for a tangy kick. Stir gently to combine all the ingredients.

This Ginger and Turmeric Tea Blend can be enjoyed hot or cold, depending on your preference. Pour it over ice for a refreshing summer drink or cozy up with a warm cup during the colder months. You can also experiment with different variations by adding a slice of lemon or a sprig of mint for an extra burst of flavour.

Not only is this tea blend a perfect choice for tea lovers, but it is also an excellent option for parents and kids who are looking for a non-alcoholic beverage that is both tasty and healthy. So, sip and savour this Ginger and Turmeric Tea Blend, and elevate your tea-drinking experience to a whole new level.

Exotic Fruit Tea Cocktails

Exotic Fruit Tea Cocktails:

If you're a tea lover, a parent looking for healthier drink choices for your kids or someone who doesn't drink alcohol, you're in for a treat! In this subchapter, titled 'Exotic Fruit Tea Cocktails Recipes', we are going to explore the world of fancy tea blends and show you how to create delightful non-alcoholic tea cocktails that will tantalize your taste buds and impress your guests.

Fancy Tea: A Guide to Non-Alcoholic Tea Cocktails

Tea is not just a comforting and relaxing beverage; it can also be transformed into a refreshing and exotic cocktail. By combining different tea varieties with vibrant fruits and other natural ingredients, you can create a wide range of flavourful and visually appealing drinks that are perfect for any occasion.

Let's start with the basics. When selecting the tea for your cocktails, opt for high-quality loose-leaf teas that are known for their unique flavours and aromas. Black teas like Earl Grey or Darjeeling can add a rich and robust base to your cocktail. Green teas such as Jasmine or Sencha provide a delicate and grassy note, while herbal teas like hibiscus or chamtomile offer a fruity and floral infusion.

Now, let's dive into some exotic fruit tea cocktail recipes. How about a Tropical Paradise Mocktail? In a shaker, combine freshly brewed hibiscus tea, pineapple juice, a splash of lime juice, and a touch of honey. Shake well and strain into a glass filled with ice. Garnish with a slice of pineapple and a sprig of mint for an extra touch of elegance.

For a refreshing twist, try the Citrus Sunrise Cooler. Steep a green tea of your choice, then let it cool. In a tall glass, muddle fresh orange slices and a few sprigs of basil. Add the cooled green tea, a splash of cranberry juice and a squeeze of lemon. Stir gently and serve over ice, garnishing with a basil leaf.

These exotic fruit tea cocktails are not only delicious but also packed with antioxidants and natural flavours. They are perfect for tea lovers, parents looking for healthier drink options for their kids or anyone who wants to enjoy a fancy loose-leaf tea experience without the alcohol.

So, next time you're hosting a gathering or simply want to treat yourself to a special drink, turn to these exotic fruit tea cocktails. Sip and savour the unique flavours and enjoy the beauty of a fancy tea transformed into a delightful mocktail. Cheers to a healthier and more vibrant tea-drinking experience!

Herbal Infusions for Mocktails

In the world of loose-leaf tea, there is a growing trend towards non-alcoholic tea cocktails, also known as mocktails. These delightful concoctions offer a refreshing and healthier alternative to traditional alcoholic beverages, making them a perfect choice for tea lovers, parents, kids and anyone looking to make healthier drink choices.

One of the key elements that elevate these mocktails to the next level is the use of herbal infusions. Herbal infusions are created by steeping various herbs and botanicals in hot water, allowing their flavours and aromas to infuse into the liquid. The result is a flavourful and fragrant concoction that serves as a base for a wide range of mocktails.

When it comes to herbal infusions, the possibilities are endless. You can experiment with different combinations to create unique and exciting flavours. For instance, a blend of chamomile, lavender, and lemon verbena creates a soothing and floral infusion, perfect for a calming mocktail. Alternatively, a mix of hibiscus, rose hips and mint delivers a vibrant and refreshing infusion that pairs well with citrus flavours.

These herbal infusions can be used as a base for mocktails by adding a variety of ingredients such as fruit juices, sparkling water or even other teas. For example, mixing a chamomile-lavender infusion with apple juice and a splash of sparkling water creates a delightful apple-lavender mocktail, which is both sweet and aromatic.

Not only do these herbal infusions add depth and complexity to mocktails, but they also offer a range of health benefits. Many herbs and botanicals used in infusions have been traditionally used for their medicinal properties. For instance, chamomile is known for its calming effects, while mint aids digestion. By incorporating these infusions into your mocktails, you can enjoy their therapeutic benefits while sipping on a delicious and refreshing beverage.

Whether you are a tea lover, a parent looking for healthier drink options for your kids or someone who simply wants to avoid alcohol, herbal infusions for mocktails are a fantastic choice. They provide an opportunity to explore the world of loose-leaf tea in a non-alcoholic way, offering unique flavours, health benefits and a refreshing alternative to traditional cocktails. So, get creative, experiment with different herbal infusions and start savouring the joys of non-alcoholic tea cocktails!

Floral Tea Elixirs

Floral tea elixirs are a delightful way for tea lovers, parents, kids and anyone who doesn't drink alcohol to indulge in loose-leaf tea while making healthier drink choices. These exquisite elixirs combine the elegance of floral flavours with the numerous health benefits of tea, creating a truly enchanting experience for your taste buds and overall well-being.

When it comes to floral tea elixirs, the possibilities are endless. You can infuse your favourite teas with delicate petals and blossoms to create a beautiful blend that will transport you to a serene garden with each sip. From the soothing aroma of lavender to the vibrant notes of rose, floral teas offer a symphony of flavours that are both refreshing and invigorating.

One of the most popular floral tea elixirs is Lavender Earl Grey. By infusing Earl Grey tea with the subtle floral essence of lavender, you create a harmonious balance that is both calming and uplifting. Served over ice with a sprig of fresh lavender, this elixir is perfect for a relaxing afternoon tea or a special gathering with friends.

Hibiscus Rose is another exquisite floral tea elixir that is both visually stunning and packed with health benefits. Hibiscus tea, known for its vibrant colour and tangy flavour, combines beautifully with the delicate aroma of rose petals. This elixir is not only refreshing but also rich in antioxidants, helping to boost your immune system and promote healthy skin.

For a unique twist on a classic, try the Chamomile Mint Blossom Elixir. The soothing properties of chamomile tea complement the refreshing taste of mint, while the addition of dried chamomile blossoms adds a touch of elegance to this drink. Served warm, this elixir is perfect for winding down after a long day or as a bedtime treat for the little ones.

Floral tea elixirs offer a healthier and alcohol-free alternative to traditional cocktails, making them suitable for people of all ages. Packed with antioxidants, vitamins and minerals, these elixirs not only satisfy your taste buds but also nourish your body, making them an ideal choice for those looking to embrace a healthier lifestyle.

So, next time you're in search of a fancy loose-leaf tea experience, look no further than floral tea elixirs. With their enticing flavours, health benefits and sheer elegance, they are sure to captivate the hearts of tea lovers, parents, kids and anyone in search of a delightful and health-conscious beverage. Sip and savour the beauty of floral tea elixirs, and let their enchantment transport you to a world of pure indulgence.

08

Chapter 8: Health Benefits of Non-Alcoholic Tea Cocktails

Antioxidant-rich Tea Varieties

Tea has been enjoyed for centuries, not only for its delightful taste but also for its numerous health benefits. In this subchapter, we explore the world of antioxidant-rich tea varieties, perfect for tea lovers, parents, kids and anyone seeking healthier drink choices.

1. Green Tea: Renowned for its high antioxidant content, green tea is a staple in many households. Packed with polyphenols, catechins and flavonoids, this variety offers a range of health benefits, including improved heart health, boosted metabolism and reduced risk of chronic diseases. Its delicate flavour makes it an excellent choice for those new to fancy tea.

2. White Tea: Known for its subtlety and delicate taste, white tea is rich in antioxidants that help protect the body from harmful free radicals. It contains catechins, theanine and polyphenols, which can aid in weight management, strengthen the immune system and promote healthy skin. White tea's mild flavour makes it perfect for kids and those looking for a milder tea experience.

3. Rooibos Tea: Originating from South Africa, rooibos tea is a caffeine-free alternative that is rich in antioxidants. Packed with various minerals and phenolic compounds, this tea variety offers anti-inflammatory properties, aids digestion and promotes relaxation. Rooibos tea's naturally

sweet taste appeals to parents and kids alike, making it an excellent choice for a healthy beverage option for the whole family.

4. Matcha Tea: Highly regarded for its vibrant green colour and unique preparation process, matcha tea is made from powdered green tea leaves. Consuming the whole leaf allows for a higher concentration of antioxidants, including catechins and chlorophyll.

Matcha offers a sustained energy boost, aids in detoxification and supports mental clarity. Its earthy flavour and versatility make it an ideal ingredient for non-alcoholic tea cocktails.

5. Herbal Infusions: While not technically tea, herbal infusions such as chamomile, peppermint and hibiscus offer a variety of health benefits. These caffeine-free options are rich in antioxidants, vitamins and minerals, promoting relaxation, aiding digestion and boosting the immune system. Herbal infusions provide an excellent alternative for individuals seeking a fancy tea experience without caffeine.

Incorporating these antioxidant-rich tea varieties into your daily routine can provide a range of health benefits for tea lovers, parents and kids alike. Whether you're looking to boost your immune system, support heart health or simply enjoy a delicious and healthy beverage, there's a loose-leaf tea option for everyone. So, sit back, sip and savour the goodness that these antioxidant-rich teas have to offer!

Digestive and Calming Properties

Tea has long been celebrated for its numerous health benefits, and one area where it truly shines is in its digestive and calming properties. Whether you're a tea lover, a parent looking for healthier drink choices for your kids, someone who doesn't consume alcohol or someone who enjoys loose- leaf tea, this subchapter is dedicated to exploring the incredible benefits of non-alcoholic tea cocktails that can soothe your stomach and provide a sense of tranquillity.

When it comes to digestion, tea has been used for centuries as a natural remedy. Many herbal teas, such as chamomile, peppermint and ginger, are well-known for their ability to ease stomach discomfort, reduce bloating and aid in digestion. By incorporating these herbs into non-alcoholic tea cocktails, you can enjoy a delicious beverage that not only tastes incredible but also helps to calm your digestive system after a meal. Imagine sipping on a refreshing peppermint and lemon tea cocktail, feeling the cooling sensation in your throat and the soothing effects in your stomach.

Additionally, tea is renowned for its calming properties. Certain teas, like lavender, lemon balm and passionflower, have gentle sedative effects that can help to reduce anxiety, promote relaxation and improve the quality of sleep. By incorporating these calming herbs into non-alcoholic tea cocktails, you can create a delightful beverage that not only tastes divine but also provides a moment of tranquillity in your busy day. Picture yourself unwinding with a lavender-infused tea cocktail, allowing the soothing aroma and flavours to wash away the stress of the day.

For parents looking for healthier drink choices for their kids, non-alcoholic tea cocktails are a fantastic option. Not only are they free from the negative effects of alcohol, but they also offer a wide range of flavours and health benefits. You can concoct a fruity hibiscus and berry tea cocktail that will delight their taste buds while providing them with antioxidants and vitamins. It's a win-win situation – a drink that is both delicious and nutritious!

In summary, non-alcoholic tea cocktails are a perfect choice for tea lovers, parents seeking healthier drink options for their kids, individuals who abstain from alcohol and those who appreciate fancy tea. With their digestive and calming properties, these delightful beverages offer a soothing experience for the stomach and the mind. So, go ahead, sip and savour the incredible benefits of these non-alcoholic tea cocktails – your taste buds and your well-being will thank you!

Boosting Energy and Immunity

In a world where health and wellness have become a top priority, it's no wonder that more and more people are turning to non-alcoholic tea cocktails as a healthier alternative. Whether you're a tea lover, a parent looking for a kid-friendly option or simply someone who doesn't drink alcohol, these fancy tea concoctions are sure to delight your taste buds while boosting your energy and immunity.

Tea has long been celebrated for its numerous health benefits, and when combined with other natural ingredients, it becomes a powerhouse of nutrients and antioxidants. One of the key benefits of tea is its ability to provide a gentle boost of energy without the crash that often accompanies caffeinated beverages.

By carefully selecting teas like green tea or yerba mate, which contain natural stimulants, you can enjoy a sustained energy lift that won't leave you feeling jittery or exhausted later on.

Additionally, many teas are known for their immune-boosting properties. Ingredients such as ginger, turmeric and lemon are commonly used in non-alcoholic tea cocktails to enhance their immune-enhancing effects. These ingredients are rich in vitamins, minerals and antioxidants that help strengthen the immune system, making you less susceptible to illnesses.

For tea lovers, the world of non-alcoholic tea cocktails opens up a whole new realm of flavours and combinations. From classic favourites like the Earl Grey Spritzer, with its delicate bergamot aroma, to innovative creations like the Matcha Mojito, which combines the earthy notes of matcha with the refreshing taste of mint, there's a tea cocktail for every palate. With a little creativity and experimentation, you can create your own signature tea cocktail that will impress even the most discerning tea connoisseurs.

Parents seeking healthier drink choices for their kids will find that non-alcoholic tea cocktails offer a guilt-free option. By replacing sugary sodas and artificial juices with these flavourful concoctions, you can introduce your children to the wonderful world of tea while ensuring they get the necessary vitamins and minerals to support their growing bodies.

So, whether you're a tea lover, a health-conscious individual or a parent looking for healthier drink choices, non-alcoholic tea cocktails are the perfect solution.

With their ability to boost energy, strengthen immunity and delight your taste buds, these fancy tea creations will become your go-to beverages for any occasion. Cheers to a healthier, more flavourful way of sipping and savouring!

Promoting Mental Well-being

In today's fast-paced world, taking care of our mental well-being has become more important than ever. The hustle and bustle of daily life can often leave us feeling overwhelmed and stressed. That's why it's crucial to prioritize self-care and find ways to relax and unwind. One of the most enjoyable and beneficial ways to do so is by indulging in the world of fancy tea.

For tea lovers, parents, kids and individuals who don't drink alcohol, exploring the realm of non-alcoholic tea cocktails can be a game-changer. Not only do these delightful concoctions offer a wide range of flavours and aromas, but they can also significantly contribute to our mental well-being.

Fancy Tea: A Guide to Non-Alcoholic Tea Cocktails

Tea, known for its calming properties, has been used for centuries to promote relaxation and alleviate stress. By incorporating various herbs and botanicals, tea can have a positive impact on our mental state. In this subchapter, we delve into the ways in which fancy tea can play a crucial role in enhancing our overall well-being.

First and foremost, the act of preparing and savouring a cup of tea can be a meditative experience in itself. Taking a moment to focus on the brewing process, inhaling the fragrant steam and finally sipping the warm elixir can help us slow down, be present and cultivate mindfulness. This simple act of self-care can have profound effects on our mental health, reducing anxiety and increasing feelings of relaxation.

Additionally, certain types of teas, such as chamomile, lavender and peppermint, are renowned for their soothing properties. These herbal infusions can help calm the mind, improve sleep quality and alleviate tension. Including these teas in our non-alcoholic tea cocktails can provide a refreshing and therapeutic experience.

Moreover, the vibrant colours and elegant presentation of fancy tea cocktails can create a sense of joy and uplift our spirits. The visual appeal of a beautifully crafted tea cocktail can elevate our mood and make us feel pampered and special.

By embracing non-alcoholic tea cocktails as a healthier drink choice, we can promote mental well-being while still indulging in the pleasure of a fancy tea experience. Whether it's a chamomile-infused mocktail, a lavender and lemon tea spritzer or a minty iced tea refresher, these delightful creations can bring a sense of serenity and balance to our lives.

In conclusion, promoting mental well-being through fancy tea is not just about the flavours and aromas; it's about creating a moment of tranquillity and self-care. By incorporating non-alcoholic tea cocktails into our daily routines, we can find solace in the simple act of sipping and savouring, fostering a healthier and happier mind.

Supporting Weight Management

In today's world, where unhealthy eating habits and sedentary lifestyles have become the norm, maintaining a healthy weight can be a challenging task. However, for all the tea lovers out there, it's time to rejoice! Tea, particularly non-alcoholic tea cocktails, can be a fantastic addition to your weight management journey. In this subchapter, we will explore the various ways in which tea can support your goals while still offering a delightful and fancy experience.

Tea is a superb choice for those seeking healthier drink alternatives. Unlike sugary beverages and alcohol, tea is virtually calorie-free, making it an excellent option for weight-conscious individuals. By replacing high-calorie options with refreshing tea cocktails, you can indulge in flavourful beverages without compromising your weight management goals.

One of the key benefits of tea is its ability to boost metabolism. Certain teas, such as green tea and oolong tea, contain compounds that can enhance fat oxidation and increase energy expenditure. By incorporating these teas into your daily routine, you can give your metabolism a natural and much-needed boost.

Furthermore, tea can be an effective appetite suppressant. The combination of warm water and natural compounds found in tea leaves can help you feel fuller for longer, reducing the temptation to snack unnecessarily. By sipping on a delicious tea cocktail between meals, you can curb cravings and maintain a healthy eating schedule.

For parents and kids alike, non-alcoholic tea cocktails offer a fantastic alternative to sugary sodas and juices. These beverages can be customized to suit individual tastes, incorporating a wide range of fruits, herbs and spices. By involving your children in the tea-making process, you can instil a love for healthy drinks from an early age, setting them up for a lifetime of good habits.

In conclusion, supporting weight management doesn't have to be a monotonous or tasteless journey. With the world of non-alcoholic tea cocktails, tea lovers, parents and individuals seeking healthier drink choices can enjoy the best of both worlds – a fancy and flavourful experience while supporting their weight management goals. So, grab your teapot, explore the diverse range of teas available and let's sip and savour our way to a healthier lifestyle.

09

Chapter 9: Hosting Tea Cocktail Parties

Setting the Ambiance

Creating the perfect ambience is an essential part of enjoying a delightful tea experience. Whether you are hosting a tea party, spending quality time with your family or simply seeking a moment of tranquillity, the right ambience can elevate your tea-drinking experience to new heights. In this subchapter, we will explore the art of setting the ambience and provide you with ideas to make your tea moments truly special.

For tea lovers, parents, kids and those who prefer non-alcoholic options, finding healthier drink choices can sometimes be a challenge. However, with the rise of fancy tea culture, there is a world of possibilities awaiting you. By incorporating these ideas into your tea sessions, you can transform them into memorable occasions.

First and foremost, choose an appropriate setting for your tea gathering. If you have a beautiful garden or a cozy living room, consider hosting your tea party there. Natural elements such as flowers, plants and sunlight can create a calming atmosphere. For indoor settings, dim the lights and light scented candles to add a touch of elegance and serenity.

Next, select the perfect tea set to enhance the overall aesthetic. Delicate porcelain cups and saucers, vintage teapots or modern glassware can all add a touch of sophistication to your tea experience. Pay attention to the details, such as having matching napkins or tablecloths, and consider using beautiful tea infusers or strainers for loose-leaf teas.

To engage your kids and make them feel included, provide them with their own special tea set. Let them choose their favourite tea flavour, and encourage them to participate in the preparations. This can be a wonderful way to introduce them to the world of tea while spending quality time together.

In addition to the physical ambience, consider adding soothing background music. Soft melodies or classical tunes can enhance relaxation and create a serene atmosphere. You might also want to offer a selection of light snacks and pastries that pair well with teas, such as scones, finger sandwiches or fruit tarts.

Remember, setting the ambience is about creating an environment that enhances your tea experience. By paying attention to the details and incorporating these ideas, you can transform your tea moments into cherished memories. So, gather your loved ones, pour a cup of your favourite tea, and let the ambience transport you to a world of tranquillity and indulgence.

Tea Cocktail Pairings with Food

As tea lovers, we understand that enjoying a delicious cup of tea goes beyond just sipping it on its own. The world of tea is vast and diverse, offering endless possibilities for pairing with different types of food to enhance the flavours and create a truly delightful experience. In this subchapter, we will explore the art of tea cocktail pairings with food, allowing you to elevate your tea-drinking experience to new heights.

For parents and kids seeking healthier drink choices, tea cocktails offer a fantastic alternative to traditional alcoholic beverages. By combining the goodness of tea with various ingredients, we can create vibrant and refreshing concoctions that are suitable for all ages. Whether it's a fruity iced tea mocktail paired with light sandwiches for a picnic or a warm spiced tea paired with cookies for a cozy evening treat, there is a tea cocktail pairing that will surely satisfy every plate.

Tea cocktails also cater to those who prefer a more sophisticated and fancy tea experience. With their unique blends of herbs, spices and fruits, these tea cocktails can be paired with an array of gourmet foods, making them perfect for special occasions and celebrations. Imagine sipping a sparkling green tea spritzer alongside a plate of delicate finger foods at your next elegant soirée. The combination of flavours and textures will leave your taste buds dancing in delight.

Moreover, for individuals seeking healthier drink choices, tea cocktails provide a guilt-free alternative to traditional sugary beverages. By using natural sweeteners like honey or agave syrup and incorporating fresh fruits and herbs, these tea cocktails offer the perfect balance of flavour without compromising on health.

From a zesty, citrus-infused iced tea paired with a light salad, to a soothing chamomile tea mixed with fresh berries and served with a wholesome bowl of granola, the possibilities for creating nutritious and delicious tea cocktail pairings are endless.

In conclusion, tea cocktail pairings with food offer a wonderful opportunity for tea lovers, parents, kids and those looking for healthier drink choices to explore the world of tea in a whole new way. From simple and refreshing mocktails to sophisticated and fancy blends, there is a tea cocktail pairing to suit every taste and occasion. So, let your creativity flow, experiment with different teas and ingredients and embark on a journey of sipping and savouring the delightful world of non-alcoholic tea cocktails. Cheers to a healthier and more flavourful tea experience!

Mocktail Stations and Bar Setups

For those who love the art of tea and are seeking healthier drink choices, mocktail stations and bar setups are the perfect addition to any gathering. Whether you are a tea lover, a parent, a child or someone who simply prefers non-alcoholic beverages, these setups offer a delightful array of loose-leaf tea options that will satisfy your taste buds and leave you feeling refreshed.

Fancy Tea: A Guide to Non-Alcoholic Tea Cocktails

Mocktail stations are a creative way to bring the concept of a traditional bar to the world of tea. Instead of alcohol, these stations are stocked with a variety of teas, syrups, fresh fruits, herbs and other ingredients that can be mixed and matched to create tantalizing tea-based concoctions. The possibilities are endless, allowing you to customize your drink to suit your preferences.

Parents will appreciate the mocktail stations as they provide a safe and enjoyable alternative for their children. Instead of serving sugary sodas or artificial juices, parents can offer their kids a range of delicious and nutritious tea mocktails. Not only will this introduce children to the world of tea, but it will also teach them about the importance of healthy drink choices from a young age.

Tea lovers will find mocktail stations to be a haven of flavour and creativity. With access to an assortment of teas, they can experiment with different combinations and create unique and exciting tea-based mocktails. From floral infusions to citrusy brews, the options are vast, and each sip will transport you to a world of tea-infused bliss.

For those who don't drink alcohol or simply prefer non-alcoholic beverages, mocktail stations are a welcome addition to any event. They provide an opportunity to socialize and enjoy a sophisticated drink without the need for alcohol. Mocktails can be just as elegant and refined as their alcoholic counterparts, making them the perfect choice for those who want to savour the experience without the side effects.

In conclusion, mocktail stations and bar setups offer a delightful way to enjoy the world of fancy tea. Whether you are a tea lover, a parent, a child or simply someone looking for healthier drink choices, these setups provide an array of options that will satisfy your taste buds and leave you feeling refreshed. So, gather your favourite ingredients and embark on a journey of tea-infused bliss at your very own mocktail station. Cheers to a world of non-alcoholic tea cocktails!

Tea Cocktails Party Themes

Tea lovers, parents, kids, people who don't drink alcohol and those on the lookout for healthier drink choices, welcome to the world of fancy tea cocktail parties! In this subchapter, we'll explore some exciting themes that will bring a touch of elegance and delight to your gatherings.

1. Garden Tea Soiree: Transform your backyard into a whimsical garden with vibrant flowers, hanging lanterns and cozy seating arrangements. Serve refreshing floral-infused tea cocktails like Lavender Lemonade Spritzer or Hibiscus Sparkler. Pair these delightful drinks with delicate finger sandwiches, scones and colourful macarons for a truly enchanting experience.

2. Vintage Tea Affair: Step back in time with a vintage-themed tea party. Set the ambience with antique teacups, lace tablecloths and soft classical music. Serve classic tea mocktails like the Earl Grey Lemon Fizz or

Mint Julep Green Tea. Accompany these timeless drinks with dainty cucumber sandwiches, buttery shortbread and delectable Victoria sponge cake.

3. Tropical Paradise Tea Escape: Bring a taste of the tropics to your tea party. Decorate the venue with vibrant colours, tropical fruits and palm leaves. Serve exotic tea cocktails such as Pineapple Mojito Iced Tea or Passionfruit Punch. Complement these refreshing drinks with tropical-inspired appetizers like coconut shrimp skewers, pineapple salsa and mango bruschetta.

4. Zen Tea Retreat: Create a serene and calming atmosphere for a peaceful tea gathering. Use minimalist décor, soft lighting and soothing music. Offer Zen-inspired tea mocktails like Matcha Mint Mojito or Citrus Zen Cooler. Pair these rejuvenating drinks with healthy tea-infused snacks like matcha energy balls, cucumber avocado rolls and green tea-infused smoothie bowls.

5. Mad Hatter's Tea Party: Embrace whimsy and eccentricity with a Mad Hatter-inspired tea party. Decorate with mismatched teacups, colourful tablecloths and quirky props. Serve playful tea mocktails such as Berry Wonderland Punch or Cheshire Cat's Chai. Accompany these delightful concoctions with a variety of mini pastries, tea sandwiches and whimsical cupcakes.

Remember, these themes are just a starting point to spark your imagination. Feel free to mix and match different elements to create your own unique tea party experience. Whether you're organizing a gathering for tea lovers, parents, kids or anyone seeking healthier drink options, these fancy tea cocktail party themes will surely leave a lasting impression. So, go ahead and let your creativity brew!

Tips for a Successful Tea Cocktail Party

If you're a tea lover, a parent or someone who doesn't drink alcohol but still loves to enjoy a fabulous beverage, then hosting a tea cocktail party is the perfect way to indulge in fancy tea creations. These non-alcoholic tea cocktails are not only delicious but also offer a healthier alternative to traditional alcoholic beverages. In this subchapter, we will provide you with some essential tips for hosting a successful tea cocktail party that will impress your guests and leave them craving for more.

1. Select a Variety of Teas: To cater to different taste preferences, offer a diverse selection of teas. Choose a combination of black, green, herbal and floral teas to provide a range of flavours and aromas. This will allow your guests to try different tea cocktails and find their favourites.

2. Experiment with Flavours: Get creative with your tea cocktails by adding various flavours and ingredients. Consider using fresh fruits, herbs, spices and even honey to enhance the taste and presentation of your drinks. Experiment with different combinations to create unique and refreshing tea cocktails.

3. Presentation is Key: Make your tea cocktail party fancy by paying attention to the presentation. Use elegant teapots, teacups and saucers to serve your beverages. Garnish each drink with a slice of fruit, a sprig of mint or a colourful straw to add a touch of sophistication.

4. Offer Mocktail Options for Kids: If you're hosting a family-friendly tea cocktail party, ensure you have mocktail options for the little ones. Create fun and vibrant tea-based mocktails that are visually appealing and delicious. Use colourful straws and fancy glasses to make the experience special for the kids.

5. Provide Tea Education: Take the opportunity to educate your guests about the various teas you're serving. Offer a brief description of each tea's origin, flavour profile and health benefits. This will not only enhance their appreciation for the tea cocktails but also make the event more engaging and educational.

6. Serve Tea-Infused Snacks: Complement your tea cocktails with a selection of tea-infused snacks. Consider serving tea-infused pastries, sandwiches or even tea-infused chocolates. This will create a cohesive tea experience and provide your guests with a delicious variety of treats.

By following these tips, you can host a memorable and successful tea cocktail party. Your guests, whether they are tea lovers, parents or individuals seeking healthier drink choices will appreciate the effort you put into creating a delightful and sophisticated tea experience. Sip and savour the flavours, and enjoy the company of your loved ones as you celebrate the joy of tea.

Chapter 10: Conclusion and Final Thoughts

Embracing the World of Non-Alcoholic Tea Cocktails

Subchapter: Embracing the World of Non-Alcoholic Tea Cocktails

Tea has always been revered for its soothing and refreshing qualities, but did you know that it can also be the star ingredient in delightful and sophisticated non-alcoholic cocktails? In this subchapter, we will explore the exciting realm of non-alcoholic tea cocktails and how they can be enjoyed by tea lovers, parents, kids, individuals who don't drink alcohol and those seeking healthier drink choices. Get ready to elevate your tea experience to new heights with these fancy tea creations.

For the tea lovers, non-alcoholic tea cocktails offer a unique way to savour the flavours of their favourite brews. Imagine a Hibiscus Mojito, where the tartness of hibiscus tea is infused with fresh mint and lime, creating a refreshing and vibrant mocktail that will leave you craving more. Or perhaps a Matcha Margarita, blending the earthy notes of matcha tea with zesty lime and a touch of sweetness, delivering a tantalizing twist on a classic cocktail.

Parents will appreciate the versatility of non-alcoholic tea cocktails as they can be enjoyed by the whole family. Gone are the days of feeling left out while the adults indulge in fancy beverages. Instead, parents can now gather around with their kids and enjoy a Virgin Raspberry Earl Grey Fizz, combining the fruity goodness of raspberries with the fragrant essence of Earl Grey tea, topped with sparkling water for a delightful and alcohol-free treat.

Fancy Tea: A Guide to Non-Alcoholic Tea Cocktails

Individuals who choose not to consume alcohol will find solace in the world of non-alcoholic tea cocktails. These beverages offer sophistication without the buzz, allowing everyone to join in the celebration without compromising their lifestyle choices. From a refreshing Jasmine Lime Spritzer to a fragrant Lavender Lemonade, non-alcoholic tea cocktails provide an array of options for those seeking healthier drink alternatives.

And let's not forget those who are always on the lookout for healthier drink choices. Non-alcoholic tea cocktails are a perfect fit for individuals who prioritize their well-being. Packed with antioxidants and natural ingredients, these beverages can be enjoyed guilt-free. Indulge in a Blueberry Green Tea Refresher, where antioxidant-rich green tea is combined with juicy blueberries and a hint of sweetness, creating a revitalizing drink that nourishes both the body and the soul.

In this subchapter, we have only scratched the surface of the endless possibilities that non-alcoholic tea cocktails offer. So, whether you are a tea lover, a parent, someone who abstains from alcohol or simply seeking healthier alternatives, embrace this exciting world of non-alcoholic tea cocktails and sip and savour the wonders that await you. Cheers to fancy tea experiences for everyone!

Experimenting with Your Own Creations

As a tea lover, there's nothing quite as exciting as creating your own unique and refreshing tea cocktails. In this subchapter, we will dive into the world of experimenting with your own tea creations, offering a delightful twist to your daily tea rituals. Whether you're a parent looking for healthier drink choices for your kids or someone who prefers non-alcoholic beverages, this guide to non-alcoholic tea cocktails is perfect for you!

Tea is not just a beverage; it's an experience. By infusing your favourite teas with a variety of flavours, you can create a whole new range of fancy tea cocktails that are sure to impress your taste buds. From fruity blends to herbal infusions, the possibilities are endless. Let's explore some tips and ideas to help you get started on your tea mixology journey.

First and foremost, it's essential to select high-quality teas as the base for your creations. Opt for loose-leaf teas rather than tea bags, as they tend to offer more robust flavours. Green tea, black tea, white tea and herbal blends are all great options to experiment with. Once you have your base, it's time to infuse it with exciting flavours.

Consider adding fresh fruits, herbs, and spices to enhance the taste and aroma of your tea cocktails. For example, a green tea infused with mint and lime can create a refreshing mojito-inspired concoction. Or try blending black tea with strawberries and basil for a unique twist on a classic iced tea.

Additionally, don't be afraid to play with different sweeteners. While traditional cocktails often rely on sugar or simple syrup, there are healthier alternatives like honey, agave nectar or even stevia. These natural sweeteners can add a touch of sweetness without overpowering the delicate flavours of your tea.

Experimenting with temperature and brewing techniques can also elevate your tea cocktails. For instance, cold-brewing your tea overnight can result in a smoother and mellower flavour profile. On the other hand, steeping your tea at a higher temperature for a shorter duration can yield a more robust and intense taste.

Lastly, presentation is key when it comes to loose-leaf tea cocktails. Serve your creations in elegant glassware, garnish with fresh herbs or fruit slices and consider adding a touch of sparkle with a splash of sparkling water or soda.

Whether you're hosting a tea party, looking for a refreshing drink for your kids or simply seeking healthier beverage choices, experimenting with your own tea creations is a delightful way to elevate your tea-drinking experience. So grab your favourite teas, let your imagination run wild and embark on a journey of flavour exploration with non-alcoholic tea cocktails. Cheers to a world of endless possibilities!

Savoring the Joy of Sipping Tea Cocktails

In a world where cocktails have become synonymous with alcohol, it's refreshing to discover a new and exciting trend that caters to both tea lovers and those who prefer non-alcoholic beverages. Welcome to the world of tea cocktails – a delightful fusion of flavours, creativity and health-conscious choices.

For tea lovers, there is nothing quite as satisfying as sipping on a warm cup of their favourite blend. But what if we told you that you could take your tea experience to a whole new level with tea cocktails? These innovative concoctions combine the aromatic goodness of tea with a variety of ingredients, resulting in a symphony of flavours that will leave your taste buds tingling.

Parents, kids and those who choose not to consume alcohol can finally revel in the joy of sipping on a fancy tea cocktail. Imagine the excitement on your child's face when they are presented with a vibrant and colourful beverage that mirrors the sophistication of an adult cocktail, without the alcohol content. These tea cocktails not only offer a delightful treat for kids but also provide a healthier alternative to sugary sodas and juices.

Tea cocktails cater to a wide range of tastes and preferences. Whether you prefer a bold and robust black tea, a soothing and aromatic herbal infusion or a delicate and floral green tea, there is a perfect cocktail waiting to be discovered. From traditional recipes to innovative blends, this book, 'Fancy Tea: A Guide to Non-Alcoholic Tea Cocktails', will take you on a journey through the world of loose-leaf tea.

The health benefits of tea are well-known, and tea cocktails embrace this aspect by incorporating fresh fruits, herbs, and natural sweeteners. These beverages offer a guilt-free indulgence, providing you with a burst of antioxidants, vitamins and minerals. Sip on a tea cocktail, and you'll not only enjoy a refreshing and delicious drink but also reap the numerous health benefits that tea has to offer.

So, whether you're a tea aficionado, a parent seeking healthier drink choices for your kids or someone simply looking for a non-alcoholic, loose-leaf tea experience, 'Fancy Tea: A Guide to Non-Alcoholic Tea Cocktails' has something for you. Get ready to tantalize your taste buds and embark on a delightful journey of tea-infused mixology. Savour the joy of sipping tea cocktails and discover a world of flavours that will leave you longing for more.

11

Appendix:

Glossary of Tea Terms

Tea, with its rich history and diverse flavours, has an entire vocabulary of its own. Whether you are a seasoned tea lover or just starting your journey into the world of tea, understanding the terminology can enhance your appreciation and enjoyment of this delightful beverage. In this glossary of tea terms, we will explore the key words and phrases that every tea enthusiast should know.

1. Camellia Sinensis: The botanical name for the tea plant, from which all true teas are derived. This plant species is responsible for the wide variety of tea types, including black, green, white, oolong, and more.

2. Infusion: The process of steeping tea leaves in water to extract their flavours and aromas. The infusion time varies depending on the type of tea and personal preference.

3. Tisane: Also known as herbal tea or infusion, tisanes are beverages made from the infusion of herbs, fruits, flowers or other plant materials. Unlike true teas, tisanes do not contain leaves from the Camellia Sinensis plant.

4. Steep: The act of allowing tea leaves or tisanes to soak in hot water for a specific period to extract their flavours. Steeping time and temperature can greatly impact the taste and strength of the tea.

5. Terroir: A French term used to describe the environmental factors that influence the taste and quality of tea, such as the soil, climate, altitude and geographical location where the tea is grown.

6. Astringency: A desirable characteristic in some teas, particularly black and oolong, which refers to the dry, puckering sensation in the mouth caused by tannins. Astringency adds complexity and depth to the tea's flavour profile.

7. Infuser: A device or tea accessory used to hold loose tea leaves or herbs during the steeping process. Infusers come in various forms, including tea balls, tea filters and tea strainers.

8. Gongfu Tea Ceremony: A traditional Chinese tea ceremony characterized by its precise brewing techniques and attention to detail. It emphasizes multiple short infusions to extract the full flavour from high-quality teas.

9. Matcha: A finely ground green tea powder that is whisked with hot water, resulting in a vibrant, frothy beverage. Matcha is celebrated for its distinctive flavour and high concentration of antioxidants.

10. Chai: A spiced tea beverage originating from India, typically made with a blend of black tea, milk, and a combination of spices such as cinnamon, cardamom, ginger, and cloves.

As tea lovers, parents, and individuals seeking healthier drink choices, understanding these tea terms will empower you to explore the world of tea with confidence. Whether you're hosting a fancy tea party or simply enjoying a quiet moment with a cup of tea, the knowledge gained from this glossary will enhance your appreciation for the art and science of tea.

Resources for Tea Ingredients and Accessories

For all the tea lovers out there, this subchapter will introduce you to a world of resources for tea ingredients and accessories that will enhance your tea-drinking experience. Whether you are

Fancy Tea: A Guide to Non-Alcoholic Tea Cocktails

a parent looking for healthier drink choices for your kids or someone who doesn't drink alcohol, this guide is perfect for you. Additionally, if you are someone who enjoys the finer things in life and appreciates the art of fancy tea, this subchapter will be your go-to resource.

When it comes to tea ingredients, sourcing high-quality tea leaves is essential. Look for online tea retailers that specialize in premium loose-leaf teas. These retailers often have a wide range of tea varieties, including black, green, white, oolong and herbal teas. Some even offer unique blends and flavoured teas to add a touch of excitement to your tea cocktails. The key is to find organic and ethically sourced teas to ensure you are getting the best quality ingredients.

To take your tea experience to the next level, invest in proper tea accessories. Teapots, tea infusers and tea strainers are essential tools for brewing tea. Choose teapots made from high-quality materials such as glass, ceramic or cast iron, as they will enhance the flavour and aroma of your tea. Tea infusers and strainers come in various shapes and sizes, allowing you to steep your loose-leaf teas effortlessly.

Look for accessories that match your personal style and elevate the overall aesthetic of your tea-drinking experience.

In addition to tea leaves and accessories, consider exploring specialty stores that offer unique tea ingredients. These can include dried flowers, herbs, spices, and even fruits that can be added to your tea cocktails to create exciting flavour profiles.

Experiment with ingredients like lavender, rose petals, cinnamon sticks and citrus peels to create your own signature tea cocktails.

Furthermore, online communities and forums dedicated to tea lovers are excellent resources to connect with like-minded individuals. These platforms provide opportunities to share ideas, recipes, and recommendations for tea ingredients and accessories. Engaging with fellow tea enthusiasts will not only expand your knowledge but also inspire you to try new tea combinations and experiment with different brewing techniques.

Remember, the journey of discovering tea ingredients and accessories is an ongoing process. Continuously explore new resources, experiment with different flavours, and share your experiences with others. With the right ingredients and accessories, you can create beautiful and delicious tea cocktails that will impress both you and your guests. So, dive into the world of fancy tea and elevate your tea-drinking experience to new heights!

Tea Cocktail Recipes Index

Welcome to the Tea Cocktail Recipes Index, a treasure trove of delightful and refreshing non-alcoholic tea cocktail recipes! In this subchapter of 'Sip and Savour: A Guide to Non-Alcoholic Tea Cocktails', we have curated a collection of fancy tea cocktails that will tantalize your taste buds and quench your thirst in the most exquisite way.

For all the tea lovers out there, this index is a dream come true. Whether you are a connoisseur or just beginning to explore the world of tea, these recipes offer a perfect blend of flavours and aromas that will transport you to a tea paradise. And the best part is, these tea cocktails are suitable for everyone, including parents, kids and those who choose not to consume alcohol.

In today's health-conscious world, it's essential to make mindful choices when it comes to beverages. Our tea cocktail recipes offer a healthier alternative to traditional cocktails without compromising on taste or sophistication. By using a variety of teas, fresh fruits, herbs, and natural sweeteners, you can enjoy a guilt-free and refreshing beverage that is both vibrant and nourishing.

From classic combinations like Earl Grey and citrus to more innovative blends like matcha and coconut, our index covers a wide range of flavours to suit every palate. Each recipe is carefully crafted to ensure the perfect balance of tea essence, sweetness and tanginess, creating a harmonious symphony of flavours with every sip.

Fancy Tea: A Guide to Non-Alcoholic Tea Cocktails

Whether you are hosting a tea party, looking for an afternoon pick-me-up or simply seeking a beverage to complement your meal, our tea cocktail recipes are sure to impress. The index provides step-by-step instructions, accompanied by beautiful photographs, guiding you through the process of creating these visually stunning and delicious concoctions.

So grab your favourite teapot, gather your loved ones and embark on a journey of tea-infused delight with our Tea Cocktail Recipes Index. Discover the magic that happens when tea blends with other ingredients to create tantalizing flavours that will leave you craving for more. Cheers to a healthier, tastier and more sophisticated way of enjoying tea!

About Tanja Boldt

Hello there, fellow book lovers!

My name is Tanja, and I am your 'Fancy Tea' book creator. Hailing all the way from Germany, I now call the beautiful landscapes of South Australia my home. In my previous life, I spent over two decades immersed in the retail industry. But when my daughter entered this world, everything changed. I embarked on a journey of personal transformation, becoming a full-time mom and diving headfirst into the world of loose-leaf tea.

You see, I was on a quest to find a beverage that not only nourished my body but also delighted my senses and uplifted my spirits, no matter the time of day. And so, armed with a passion for art and beauty, I began experimenting with herbs and dried fruits, blending them in ways that created wonderfully aromatic teas bursting with health benefits.

Driven by my love for all things tea, I birthed the brainchild that is Jaroma Tea - a loose-leaf tea business that aims to bring you a sensory adventure with every sip.

As the summer heat rolled in, I found myself concocting refreshing and healthy iced tea creations for my loved ones using our premium loose-leaf tea as a base. And now, I am thrilled to share these tantalizing recipes with everyone, inviting you to discover just how adventurous loose-leaf tea can be.

So, whether you're curled up with a captivating novel, exploring the pages of a non-fiction masterpiece or simply seeking a moment of tranquillity in a chaotic world, allow me to introduce you to a world of tea that not only nourishes your body but also uplifts your soul. Let's embark on this tea-infused journey together, one sip at a time.

Cheers to a life filled with the magic of books and the serenity of a well-steeped cup of tea!

www.ingramcontent.com/pod-product-compliance
Lightning Source LLC
Chambersburg PA
CBHW042303150426
43196CB00005B/60